Introduction to:

Muhammad (ﷺ)
The Prophet of Mercy

Muhammad's Role in Islam

By Jalal Abualrub
Edited by Alaa Mencke

ISBN: 0-9703766-8-5
Madinah Publishers and Distributors
www.IslamLife.com; IslamLife@Gmail.com

First Edition
Copyright © June 2007

All rights for this book are reserved for **Madinah Publishers and Distributors** and its owners **Jalal Abualrub** and **Alaa Mencke**.

Without prior written permission from the Publisher, i.e., **Madinah Publishers and Distributors**, no part of this book may be utilized, copied or reproduced in any way or form or by any means, electronic or mechanical, including recording and photocopying, or by any retrieval systems and information storage.

الطبعة الأولى ربيع الثاني 1424 هـ...الموافق يونيو 2007 م

كافة حقوق الطبع والنشر والتوزيع لهذا الكتاب تعود لشركة "المدينة للطباعة والنشر" لصاحبيها جلال أبو الرُب وآلاء منكي.

لا يسمح بإعادة طبع أو تصوير أو بث هذا الكتاب بأي وسيلة كانت أو باستخدام الكمبيوتر أو غير ذلك من وسائط البث والتصوير بدون إذن مسبق كتابي من "المدينة للطباعة والنشر".

ISBN: 0-9703766-8-5
Madinah Publishers and Distributors
www.IslamLife.com; IslamLife@Gmail.com

Table of Contents

Introduction to *Muhammad* (ﷺ), *The Prophet of Mercy*: Muhammad's Role in Islam 5

The *Quran* and *Sunnah*: Islam's Two Resources 6

A Brief Description of the Series of Books Titled: *The Prophet of Mercy* ...9

The Prophet of Mercy (ﷺ): Muhammad's Role in Islam 12

    First: Allah (ﷻ) is the One and Only Creator, Lord, Protector and Sustainer of all existence...12

    Second: Allah (ﷻ) is described with the Most Beautiful Names and Perfect Attributes..14

    Third: None has the right to be worshipped, except Allah (ﷻ); Allah (ﷻ) created creation to worship Him Alone, without partners 15

    Fourth: To Allah (ﷻ), *the* religion is Islam 17

    Fifth: Allah (ﷻ) chooses Messengers from angels and from mankind to convey His Messages to His Creation 17

    Sixth: Jibreel (Gabriel ﷺ) is Allah's Angel Messenger to His Human Messengers 17

    Seventh: Human Messengers convey *Tau'heed*, i.e., Allah's Islamic Monotheism, establish practices of worship, permissible dealings and good conduct; they also deliver Allah's Promises and Warnings 19

    Eighth: Allah (ﷻ) sent a prophet to every nation that existed.....................21

    Ninth: Allah (ﷻ) sent down Divine Books to His Messengers and revealed Prophetic *Sunnah* Traditions (Law) to them 22

    Tenth: Allah (ﷻ) mentioned twenty-five of His Messengers in the *Quran*, five of whom had the strongest of will............................22

    Eleventh: Muhammad (ﷺ), Allah's Final and Last Messenger and Prophet 23

    Twelfth: The coming of Muhammad (ﷺ) was announced in the Books Allah revealed to earlier prophets and by their words 24

    Thirteenth: Muhammad's Message is universal.................................27

Fourteenth: Muhammad (ﷺ) came to testify to the truth of Allah's Messengers who came before him, resurrect a part of their law and purify their image from the slanders that were added to their legacies 28

Fifteenth: Muhammad (ﷺ) came to re-establish the same Message of *Tau`heed*, Allah's Islamic Monotheism, that Allah (ﷻ) revealed to every prophet and messenger He sent before him..29

Sixteenth: The *Quran* praises Prophet Muhammad's standard of character 31

Seventeenth: The *Quran* asserts Prophet Muhammad's compassionate eagerness to benefit mankind..32

Eighteenth: Prophet Muhammad (ﷺ) received the *Quran* from Allah (ﷻ) testifying to the truth contained within Books Allah (ﷻ) revealed to earlier prophets and overruling them with regards to the Law.....................33

Nineteenth: The *Quran* was not the only revelation sent from Allah (ﷻ) to Prophet Muhammad (ﷺ); Muhammad's Prophetic *Sunnah* is also Divine Revelation..34

Twentieth: In the *Quran*, Allah (ﷻ) explained why He made a promise to teach Prophet Muhammad (ﷺ) the *Quran* and its *Bayan* (explanation) 36

Twenty-First: The *Quran* and Prophetic *Sunnah* explain the Pillars of *Eman*, meaning, the Islamic Faith 36

Twenty-Second: The *Quran* and the Prophetic *Sunnah* explain the practical Pillars of Islam..37

Twenty-Third: Necessity of ruling by what Allah revealed 39

Twenty-Fourth: The *Quran* declares that Islam is life.................................40

Twenty-Fifth: Allah (ﷻ) completed and perfected Islam; Islam is a complete way of life that is to be taken as a whole 40

Twenty-Sixth: Islam rejects all types of innovation in religion 41

Twenty-Seventh: The *Quran* identifies Prophet Muhammad (ﷺ) as the example to follow 42

Twenty-Eighth: In the *Quran*, Allah (ﷻ) ordered Muslims to refer to Muhammad (ﷺ) for judgment if they fall into any type of dispute.............43

Twenty-Ninth: Allah (ﷻ) did not give the believers the option to choose which part of His Revelation they want to abide by 44

Thirtieth: Allah (ﷻ) made earning His Love conditional upon the *Ittiba`*, the following of and obedience to His Prophet (ﷺ) 44

Thirty-First: In the *Quran*, Allah (ﷻ) made referring to His Prophet's judgment in every dispute or difference that arises between Muslims the sign that distinguishes *Eman* (Faith) 45

Thirty-Second: Whoever obeys the Prophet's commandments obeys Allah Himself; whoever disobeys the Prophet's commandments disobeys Allah Himself..................45

Thirty-Third: The *Quran* gives a clear example of the consequence of defying the Prophet's *Amr*, his commandments and *Sunnah* Traditions 46

Thirty-Fourth: The *Quran* warns against hypocrisy manifested by rejecting referring to the Prophet (ﷺ) for judgment..................47

Thirty-Fifth: The *Quran* orders all Muslims to follow the faith in the method of the companions of Muhammad (ﷺ)..................48

Thirty-Sixth: Allah (ﷻ) promised to protect the *Dhikr* from corruption, by protecting every letter of the *Quran* in addition to its *Bayan* (meaning; explanation; implication)..................53

Thirty-Seventh: *Dhikr* comprises of the *Quran* and the Prophet's *Sunnah*, the *Quran*'s practical *Bayan*..................53

Thirty-Eighth: The *Sunnah* includes the *Quran*'s practical *Bayan* (meaning), the same *Bayan* that Allah (ﷻ) promised to teach His Prophet (ﷺ) so he could teach it to others..................54

    Conclusion: In the *Quran*, Allah (ﷻ) asserted the significance of His Prophet's *Sunnah* in various ways and in numerous instances..................55

Thirty-Ninth: By Allah's Permission, Prophet Muhammad (ﷺ) established the Islamic *Sharee`ah* (Law)..................57

Fortieth: As promised, Allah (ﷻ) protected the *Quran* from corruption in various ways..................71

    Abu Bakr Ibn Abi Qu'hafah (ؓ): The First to Collect the *Quran* in One Manuscript..................72

    Umar Ibn al-Khattab (ؓ): The First to Suggest Collecting the *Quran* in One Manuscript..................76

    Uthman Ibn `Affan (ؓ): Collector of the *Quran* in One Universal Manuscript..................76

    Old Arabic Script as Compared to Current Uthmani Script..................79

Forty-First: Allah (ﷻ) protected the Islamic Message, *Quran* and *Sunnah*, from corruption; His Prophet (ﷺ) completely and entirely delivered Allah's Message and explained it perfectly..80

Forty-Second: Numerous books on the *Quran's Tafsir* (meaning) and *Hadeeth* Collections explain the meaning contained in the *Quran*; *Tafsir* and *Hadeeth* books preserve the *Quran's* letter and also its *Bayan* (meaning) from corruption..81

Forty-Third: The *Quran* was revealed in seven '*A`hruf* (Pl. for 'Harf', i.e., way, dialect)', *all taught by the Prophet himself* who was sent with both the *Quran* and its *Bayan* (meaning)..83

    Examples to *A`hruf*..84

Forty-Fourth: The Prophet's companions (ﷺ) agreed on collecting the *Quran* in one unified manuscript..84

    Points of interest on this topic..85

Forty-Fifth: An example of *Tafsir-ul-Quran*..93

Forty-Sixth: Allah (ﷻ) protected the *Sunnah* from corruption..96

Forty-Seventh: Numerous *Hadeeth* Collections recorded and transcribed the Prophet's *Sunnah*, and thus, preserved the *Sunnah* from corruption.....98

Forty-Eighth: *Isnad* is a superb scientific method with which the Muslim Nation can and did preserve the letter and the meaning of Islam's two resources, the *Quran* and the *Sunnah*..101

    A Rare *Hadeeth* Narration..101

Forty-Ninth: *Sahih al-Bukhari*; Example of *Sunnah* Collections..104

    Bukhari's Biography..105

    Al-Jami` as-Sahih (*Sahih al-Bukhari*)..109

    An Example of Bukhari's *Hadeeth* Narrations..109

Fiftieth: This is the legacy of Muhammad (ﷺ); what this book contains is only part of why Muslims love and respect Muhammad (ﷺ) more than they love and respect any other human being..111

List of References..116

    Selected Books Translated by Jalal Abualrub..118

Introduction to:

Muhammad (ﷺ) The Prophet of Mercy

Muhammad's Role in Islam

This is an introduction to an eight-book series titled, *The Prophet of Mercy*, explaining why Allah (ﷻ[1]) said these words about Muhammad (ﷺ[2]) in the *Quran*,

$$﴿ وَمَآ أَرْسَلْنَٰكَ إِلَّا رَحْمَةً لِّلْعَٰلَمِينَ ﴾$$

{*And We have sent you* (O, Muhammad ﷺ) *not but as a mercy for the 'Âlamîn* (all that exists)} (21:107).

Muhammad, peace be upon him, is Islam's Prophet and its most important person. Through the *Quran*, Islam's Holy Book, and his *Sunnah*, or Prophetic Traditions, and his status as a Legislator by Allah's Permission, Prophet Muhammad (ﷺ)

---

[1] [ﷻ (*Sub`hanahu wa-ta`ala*): This statement is recited after mentioning Allah's Name; translated, it means, 'He (Allah) is Glorified and Exalted.' There are other statements of glorification Muslims recite upon mentioning Allah's Name.]

[2] [ﷺ (*Salla-llahu `alaihi wa-sallam*): This statement is recited after mentioning Prophet Muhammad; it means, 'May Allah's Peace and Blessings be upon him'.]

established Islam's religious, social, political, economic and educational systems. Muhammad (ﷺ) is also the ultimate example of how a Muslim should be, and all Muslims are required to strive and emulate his *Sunnah* practices and standard of character.

The *Quran* and *Sunnah*: Islam's Two Resources

Islam is built on two resources, the *Quran*, the Muslims' Holy Book, and the *Sunnah*, or Muhammad's Prophetic Traditions.

***Quran*:** The literal Word of Allah (ﷻ), Creator of everything. The *Quran* contains description of Allah (ﷻ), details of the Islamic Faith, news of the past, the future and the Unseen, and general rulings regulating aspects of life and religion, including the Islamic code of conduct and behavior.[3]

***Sunnah*:** Muhammad's Prophetic Traditions. The *Sunnah*, the practical explanation and implementation of the *Quran*, emphasizes the Islamic Faith as stated in the *Quran*, establishes the specific methods of religious practices and legislates for Muslims their dealings, acts of worship and Islamic conduct.

Even though one-fifth of humanity embraces Islam today and strives to emulate Islam's Prophet, Muhammad (ﷺ), most of mankind still does not have adequate access to the legacy of the man himself, his actions, his standard of character or the essence of his religion. Many Muslims are also generally unaware of many of these aspects which makes this series more needed and necessary.

This introduction to, *The Prophet of Mercy*, includes a detailed description of the significance of Muhammad (ﷺ) with regards to Islam and Muslims; it is heavily based on Islam's Holy Book, the *Quran*. Understanding the significance of the Prophet of Islam (ﷺ)

---

[3] [There are **6236** *Ayat* in the *Quran* each called, *Ayah* ('Sentence', or less accurately, 'verse'); there are **114** *Surahs* (chapters) in the *Quran* (Saqr, Abdul Badee` (1992). *At-Tajweedu wa-`Ulumu al-Quran* (Pg., 20-21).]

Introduction to: Muhammad (ﷺ), The Prophet of Mercy

with regards to the Islamic Faith is essential for those who seek to understand the religion itself, the role of Islamic Law in the life of Muslims, the events that shaped the early era of Islam, the obedience Prophet Muhammad (ﷺ) enjoyed from his companions (ﷺ[4]) and the deep respect he has in the hearts of the believers.

In addition, before this series, *The Prophet of Mercy*, details Prophet Muhammad's *Seerah* (biography), it is essential to first establish his role in Islam so that the subsequent narratives of his biography and details of his actions are studied more carefully and taken more seriously by the readers -hence this introduction.

Muslims also need this introduction. Allah willing, the more Muslims learn about the religious significance of their Prophet's *Sunnah*, the more likely they will strive and seek knowledge in it, abide by its commandments and patiently preach it to others, as much as they can. The more Muslims acquire knowledge in the specifics of the *Sunnah*, the more important the Prophet's actions and how he explained Islam in practice will become to them. This will also help Muslims be good ambassadors for Islam on behalf of Muhammad (ﷺ), by acting upon the *Sunnah* and refraining from contradicting it or defying its Law. Allah willing, they will also become sincere followers of Prophet Muhammad (ﷺ) so as to earn Allah's Pleasure, live a happy life and expect a happier Hereafter.

Allah willing, this introduction will be simple and straightforward explaining various concepts and articles of faith by quoting parts of the *Quran, Sunnah* or both so as to bring examples that explain the concept under discussion. Thus, this book will largely be self-explanatory, brief and to the point, Allah willing.

The Arabic original of the Quranic and Prophetic Statements is included in all eight books in this series, followed by the English translation of the meaning of the quoted texts; all original resources

---

[4] [ﷺ, or, 'Radhiya-llahu `anhum': This statement means, 'May Allah be pleased with them'; it is recited for the benefit of the Prophet's companions, who, as the Prophet (ﷺ) declared, are the best people (*Bukhari* [2458] and *Muslim* [4601]).]

of the *Quran* and *Sunnah* are found in Arabic. The English translation of the meaning contained in the *Quran* and the meaning of *Hadeeths* found in *Sahih al-Bukhari* are mainly taken from the works of Dr. Muhammad Taqi-ud-Deen al-Hilali and Dr. Muhammad Mu`hsin Khan.

It should be stated here that the author of this series has also benefited to a good extent from the efforts of Shaikh Alawi Ibn Abdul Qadir as-Saqqaf, who established a beneficial website (www.Dorar.net) that lists tens of thousands of *Hadeeths* along with the judgment on each *Hadeeth* by *Hadeeth* Scholars with regards to authenticity or lack of it. *Following is a brief description of the eight books contained in this series.*

We end our speech by saying: All thanks and praises are due to Allah (ﷻ); and may Allah's Peace and Blessings be on all of His Prophets and Messengers, such as and foremost among them Adam (عليه السلام[5]), Nu`h (Noah عليه السلام), Ibrahim (Abraham عليه السلام), Musa (Moses عليه السلام), `Esa (Jesus عليه السلام), and ending with Muhammad (ﷺ).

Jalal Abualrub
June 15th, 2007

Madinah Publishers and Distributors
www.IslamLife.com; IslamLife@gmail.com

---

[5] [عليه السلام, or, "**Alaihi as-salam**': This statement, which means, 'Peace be upon him', is recited upon mentioning the prophets and the angels.]

A Brief Description of the Eight-Book Series Titled:
The Prophet of Mercy

Introduction to, The Prophet of Mercy: This book concentrates on describing Muhammad's significance to Islam and Muslims, by using Quranic and *Sunnah* evidence defining his Prophetic role and introducing him to mankind. This book, along with the Prophet's brief Seerah (biography), soon to follow, Allah willing, will benefit both Muslim and non-Muslim readers by offering them the opportunity to know Prophet Muhammad (ﷺ) and his role in Islam.

❈❈❈

50 'New' Righteous and Humane Aspects Brought by Muhammad (ﷺ), the Prophet of Mercy: This is a direct response to Pope Benedict XVI's assertion that if one looks at the legacy of Muhammad (ﷺ), one will only find evil and inhuman aspects. This book mentions more than **50** different aspects of Islam that are both righteous and humane according to sound mind and uncorrupt religion.

❈❈❈

Glad Tidings in the Two Testaments About the Coming of Muhammad (ﷺ): The Prophets who came before Muhammad (ﷺ), including Jesus Christ, peace be upon him, brought *Basha-ir*, or glad tidings, about the coming of Muhammad (ﷺ). This book expounds on the glad tidings contained in the *Two Testaments* concerning the coming of Muhammad (ﷺ) and compares them to various Quranic and Prophetic Texts on the same topic. Read what the Messiah Jesus (ﷺ) said about Muhammad (ﷺ) being the Sent as Allah's Final and Last Prophet and Messenger.

❈❈❈

***Holy Wars, Crusades, Jihad*; 2nd edition:** Presently, much of the criticism directed at Prophet Muhammad (ﷺ) is concentrated on the rulings of warfare in Islam. This is a needed and necessary scientific research for those, including Muslims, who wish to know what Islam really legislates on aspects of war and peace.

❊❊❊

***Biography of, The Prophet of Mercy*: This is** a brief *Seerah* (biography) of Prophet Muhammad (ﷺ) taken from hundreds of resources; brief in size, but an enormous work requiring extensive research. It will be straightforward and easy to read with few intensive footnotes, Allah willing.

❊❊❊

***Muhammad* (ﷺ)*, The Prophet of Mercy; An Intimate Portrait*:** This book will contain a detailed description of the man himself, Muhammad (ﷺ), Allah's Prophet, his qualities, the way he conducted himself in the religion, how he was as a father, friend, teacher, *Zahid*[6], worshipper of Allah, *Mujahid*, husband, political leader, etc., and how he established everything we call 'Islam.' This unique book describes the Prophet (ﷺ) beyond *Seerah* (biography) stories as it reveals his qualities and exceptional character.

❊❊❊

***Muhammad* (ﷺ)*, the Warrior Prophet*:** A great deal of misinformation surrounds the establishment of the Islamic State. This book contains detailed description of how the Islamic State was founded; a narrative of all Prophetic battles; a count of all casualties, Muslim and otherwise; a comparison between the *Quran* and the *Two Testaments* with regards to rulings of warfare.

❊❊❊

---

[6] [*Zuhd* pertains to modesty and humble living; a *Zahid* practices *Zuhd*.]

101 Doubts about Islam and Rebuttal: Each doubt will be rebutted in 3-5 pages and will contain detailed positive and negative comparisons between the *Two Testaments* and the *Quran* and Muhammad's *Sunnah*.

❁❁❁

Allah willing, these books will be in print within 18-24 months of the publication of this book. Some of these books will later be read onto CDs, Allah willing, to make the books more accessible to a wider audience. This effort is made in pursuit of the Truth, to truly explain Muhammad (ﷺ) to the world. In this perspective, this series is far more than defending the Prophet (ﷺ) against attack on his actions and legacy. This series is, and as its title states and indicates, about Muhammad (ﷺ), *The Prophet of Mercy*.

Jalal Abualrub
June 15th, 2007.

Madinah Publishers and Distributors
www.IslamLife.com; IslamLife@gmail.com

﷽

In the name of Allah, Most Gracious, Most Merciful

The Prophet of Mercy (ﷺ) Muhammad's Role in Islam

First: Allah (ﷻ) is the One and Only Creator, Lord, Protector and Sustainer of all existence.

Allah (ﷻ) said in the *Quran*,

﴿ ذَٰلِكُمُ ٱللَّهُ رَبُّكُمْ لَآ إِلَٰهَ إِلَّا هُوَ خَٰلِقُ كُلِّ شَىْءٍ ﴾

{*Such is Allâh, your Lord! Lâ ilâha illa Huwa* (none has the right to be worshipped but He), *the Creator of all things.*} (6:102 [i.e., *Surah* or Quranic chapter number 6, *Ayah* number 102])

Allah (ﷻ) also said,

﴿ قُلْ هُوَ ٱللَّهُ أَحَدٌ ۝ ٱللَّهُ ٱلصَّمَدُ ۝ لَمْ يَلِدْ وَلَمْ يُولَدْ ۝ وَلَمْ يَكُن لَّهُۥ كُفُوًا أَحَدٌۢ ۝ ﴾

Introduction to: Muhammad (ﷺ), The Prophet of Mercy

{*Say* (O, Muhammad ﷺ): *"He is Allâh, (the) One. Allâh-us-Samad⁷. He begets not, nor was He begotten. And there is none co-equal or comparable unto Him."*} (112:1-3)

Prophet Muhammad (ﷺ) said,

" كَانَ اللَّهُ وَلَمْ يَكُنْ شَيْءٌ قَبْلَهُ وَكَانَ عَرْشُهُ عَلَى الْمَاءِ ثُمَّ خَلَقَ السَّمَوَاتِ وَالأَرْضَ وَكَتَبَ فِي الذِّكْرِ كُلَّ شَيْءٍ "

"There was Allah and nothing else before Him, and His Throne was over the water; afterwards He created the Heavens and the Earth and wrote everything in the Dhikr (Book of Decrees)" (Bukhari⁸ [6868]).

In one of his *Hadeeths*⁹, Prophet Muhammad (ﷺ) informed mankind about Allah's encompassing Knowledge, when he said,

" إِنَّ أَوَّلَ مَا خَلَقَ اللَّهُ الْقَلَمَ فَقَالَ اكْتُبْ فَقَالَ مَا أَكْتُبُ قَالَ اكْتُبِ الْقَدَرَ مَا كَانَ وَمَا هُوَ كَائِنٌ إِلَى الأَبَدِ "

"Right after Allah created the Pen, He said to it, 'Write!' The Pen said, 'What should I write?' Allah said, 'Write al-Qadar: what

---

⁷ [Allâh (ﷻ) — the Self-Sufficient Master, Whom all creatures need; He neither eats nor drinks]

⁸ [*Al-Jamiu` as-Sahih*, also known as, *Sahih al-Bukhari*: The collection of Prophetic *Hadeeths* (Statements) by Imam Muhammad Ibn Isma`eel al-Bukhari (194-256AH*/817-879CE). Sahih al-Bukhari is the most authentic collection of Prophetic *Hadeeths* (or Statements) and the most authentic book to Muslims after the *Quran*. *AH, means, After the *Hijrah*, i.e., after the Prophet's migration from Makkah to Madinah, which occurred in 623CE]

⁹ [*Hadeeth*: Literally, it means, 'Speech'; with regards to the Prophet (ﷺ), *Hadeeth* is in reference to his statements and reports of his actions and his agreeing to or rejecting some statements or actions.]

happened and what will happen for-ever."' (A *Sahih Hadeeth*; *Sahih at-Tirmidhi*[10] [2155])

Second: Allah (ﷻ) is described with the Most Beautiful Names and Perfect Attributes.

Allah (ﷻ) said,

﴿ وَلِلَّهِ ٱلْأَسْمَاءُ ٱلْحُسْنَىٰ فَٱدْعُوهُ بِهَا ﴾

{*And* (all) *the Most Beautiful Names belong to Allâh, so call on Him by them*} (7:180).

Allah (ﷻ) also said,

﴿ هُوَ ٱللَّهُ ٱلَّذِى لَآ إِلَٰهَ إِلَّا هُوَ عَٰلِمُ ٱلْغَيْبِ وَٱلشَّهَٰدَةِ هُوَ ٱلرَّحْمَٰنُ ٱلرَّحِيمُ ۝ هُوَ ٱللَّهُ ٱلَّذِى لَآ إِلَٰهَ إِلَّا هُوَ ٱلْمَلِكُ ٱلْقُدُّوسُ ٱلسَّلَٰمُ ٱلْمُؤْمِنُ ٱلْمُهَيْمِنُ ٱلْعَزِيزُ ٱلْجَبَّارُ ٱلْمُتَكَبِّرُ سُبْحَٰنَ ٱللَّهِ عَمَّا يُشْرِكُونَ ۝ هُوَ ٱللَّهُ ٱلْخَٰلِقُ ٱلْبَارِئُ ٱلْمُصَوِّرُ لَهُ ٱلْأَسْمَاءُ ٱلْحُسْنَىٰ يُسَبِّحُ لَهُۥ مَا فِى ٱلسَّمَٰوَٰتِ وَٱلْأَرْضِ وَهُوَ ٱلْعَزِيزُ ٱلْحَكِيمُ ۝ ﴾

---

[10] [This *Hadeeth* is from the grade *Sahih*, the higher grade of authentic *Hadeeths*, higher than *Hasan Hadeeths*.
*Jami` at-Tirmidhi*, by Imam Muhammad Ibn `Eesa at-Tirmidhi (210-279 AH/833-902), is one of the six major Collections of *Hadeeth*: The Two Sahihs by Bukhari and Muslim, and the *Sunan* Collections by Abu Dawud, at-Tirmidhi, an-Nasaii and Ibn Majah.
Sahih Sunan at-Tirmidhi, by Shaikh Nasir ad-Deen al-Albani, contains the *Sahih* (authentic) *Hadeeths* found in, *Jami` at-Tirmidhi*, while al-Albani's, *Dha`eef Sunan at-Tirmidhi*, lists the *Dha`eef* (weak) *Hadeeth* narrations found in *Jami at-Tirmidhi*.]

{He is Allâh, beside Whom Lâ ilâha illa Huwa (none has the right to be worshipped but He) the All-Knower of the Unseen and the Seen. He is the Most Gracious, the Most Merciful. He is Allâh, beside Whom Lâ ilâha illa Huwa (none has the right to be worshipped but He), the King, the Holy, the One Free from all defects, the Giver of security, the Watcher over His creatures, the All-Mighty, the Compeller, the Supreme. Glory be to Allâh! (High is He) above all that they associate as partners with Him. He is Allâh, the Creator, the Inventor of all things, the Bestower of forms. To Him belong the Best Names. All that is in the heavens and the earth glorify Him. And He is the All-Mighty, All-Wise.} (59:22-24)

Third: None has the right to be worshipped, except Allah (ﷻ); Allah (ﷻ) created creation to worship Him Alone, without partners.

Allah (ﷻ) said,

$$\text{﴿ وَمَا خَلَقْتُ ٱلْجِنَّ وَٱلْإِنسَ إِلَّا لِيَعْبُدُونِ ﴾}$$

{And I (Allâh) created not the Jinn[11] and mankind except that they should worship Me (Alone)} (51:56).

Allah (ﷻ) also said,

$$\text{﴿ ۞ وَٱعْبُدُوا۟ ٱللَّهَ وَلَا تُشْرِكُوا۟ بِهِۦ شَيْـًٔا ﴾}$$

{Worship Allâh and join none with Him (in worship)} (4:36).

In the Quran, Allah (ﷻ) reminded mankind of some of His Favors on them and of His Right on them,

---

[11] [Jinn: The devils are disbelieving Jinn; there are also believers among Jinn, who, just like mankind, have the freedom to choose between good and evil.
Allah's Prophet (ﷺ) said that the Jinn were created from fire (Muslim [5314]).]

$$\{ \text{وَمِنْ آيَاتِهِ اللَّيْلُ وَالنَّهَارُ وَالشَّمْسُ وَالْقَمَرُ ۚ لَا تَسْجُدُوا لِلشَّمْسِ وَلَا لِلْقَمَرِ وَاسْجُدُوا لِلَّهِ الَّذِي خَلَقَهُنَّ إِنْ كُنْتُمْ إِيَّاهُ تَعْبُدُونَ} \}$$

{And among His Signs are the night and the day, and the sun and the moon. Prostrate yourselves not to the sun, nor to the moon, but prostrate yourselves to Allâh Who created them, if you (really) worship Him.} (41:37)

Muhammad (ﷺ), the Prophet of Islam, said to Mu`adh Ibn Jabal (ﷺ[12]), his friend and close companion,

" هَلْ تَدْرِي حَقَّ اللَّهِ عَلَى عِبَادِهِ وَمَا حَقُّ الْعِبَادِ عَلَى اللَّهِ ... فَإِنَّ حَقَّ اللَّهِ عَلَى الْعِبَادِ أَنْ يَعْبُدُوهُ وَلَا يُشْرِكُوا بِهِ شَيْئًا وَحَقَّ الْعِبَادِ عَلَى اللَّهِ أَنْ لَا يُعَذِّبَ مَنْ لَا يُشْرِكُ بِهِ شَيْئًا "

"Do you know the right Allah has on His slaves and the right the slaves have on Allah? Allah's right on the slaves is that they should worship Him (Alone) and should not worship any besides Him. And the right the slaves have on Allah is that He should not punish those who worship none besides Him." (Bukhari [2644] and Muslim[13] [44])

---

[12] [ﷺ, or, **'Radhiya-llahu `anhu'**, means, 'May Allah be pleased with him'; it is recited for the benefit of the Prophet's individual male companions.]

[13] [*As-Sa`hi`han*: The Two Authentic Collections, *Bukhari* and *Muslim*. The Islamic Nation has agreed that *Hadeeth* Collections of Imams Muhammad Ibn Isma`eel al-Bukhari and Muslim Ibn al-`Hajjaj al-Qushairi (204-261AH/827-884CE) are the two most authentic books of *Hadeeth*, meaning, reports of Prophet Muhammad's actions and Statements. Normally, it is sufficient to say that a *Hadeeth* is found in *Sahih al-Bukhari*, *Sahih Muslim*, or both of them to indicate authenticity. As for other *Hadeeth* Collections, it is necessary to establish the authenticity of *Hadeeths* found in them, by relying on the statements of *Hadeeth* Scholars, who study the chains of narrators and texts for various *Hadeeths* to determine authenticity of the *Hadeeths* or lack of it.]

Fourth: To Allah (ﷻ), *the* religion is Islam.

Allah (ﷻ) said,

﴿ إِنَّ ٱلدِّينَ عِندَ ٱللَّهِ ٱلْإِسْلَٰمُ ﴾

{*Truly, the religion with Allâh is Islâm*} (3:19).

Allah (ﷻ) also said,

﴿ وَمَن يَبْتَغِ غَيْرَ ٱلْإِسْلَٰمِ دِينًا فَلَن يُقْبَلَ مِنْهُ وَهُوَ فِى ٱلْأَخِرَةِ مِنَ ٱلْخَٰسِرِينَ ﴾

{*And whoever seeks a religion other than Islâm, it will never be accepted of him, and in the Hereafter he will be among the losers*} (3:85).

Fifth: Allah (ﷻ) chooses Messengers from angels and from mankind to convey His Messages to His Creation.

Allah (ﷻ) said,

﴿ ٱللَّهُ يَصْطَفِى مِنَ ٱلْمَلَٰٓئِكَةِ رُسُلًا وَمِنَ ٱلنَّاسِ إِنَّ ٱللَّهَ سَمِيعٌۢ بَصِيرٌ ﴾

{*Allâh chooses Messengers from angels[14] and from men. Verily, Allâh is All-Hearer, All-Seer.*} (22:75)

Sixth: Jibreel (Gabriel ﷺ) is Allah's Angel Messenger to His Human Messengers.

In the *Quran*, Allah (ﷻ) described the job entrusted to *Ru`hu-l-Qudus*, Angel Jibreel (Gabriel ﷺ),

---

[14] [The Prophet (ﷺ) said that the angels were created from light (*Muslim* [5314]).]

Muhammad's Role in Islam

$$\left\{ قُلْ نَزَّلَهُ رُوحُ ٱلْقُدُسِ مِن رَّبِّكَ بِٱلْحَقِّ لِيُثَبِّتَ ٱلَّذِينَ ءَامَنُوا۟ وَهُدًى وَبُشْرَىٰ لِلْمُسْلِمِينَ ﴾$$

{*Say* (O, Muhammad ﷺ) *Ru`hu-l-Qudus* (Angel Jibril [Gabriel]) *has brought it* (the Qur'ân) *down from your Lord with truth, that it may make firm and strengthen* (the Faith of) *those who believe, and as a guidance and glad tidings to those who have submitted* (to Allâh as Muslims)} (16:102).

Allah (ﷻ) also said,

$$\left\{ قُلْ مَن كَانَ عَدُوًّا لِّجِبْرِيلَ فَإِنَّهُ نَزَّلَهُ عَلَىٰ قَلْبِكَ بِإِذْنِ ٱللَّهِ مُصَدِّقًا لِّمَا بَيْنَ يَدَيْهِ وَهُدًى وَبُشْرَىٰ لِلْمُؤْمِنِينَ ﴾$$

{*Say* (O, Muhammad ﷺ): "*Whoever is an enemy to Jibrâîl* (Gabriel ﷺ) (*let him die in his fury*), *for indeed he has brought it* (this *Qur'ân*) *down to your heart by Allâh's Permission, confirming what came before it* [such as, *Taurât* (original *Torah* of Moses) and *Injeel* (original *Gospel* of Jesus)] *and guidance and glad tidings for the believers*"} (2:97).

Ayah[15] 2:97 is connected to several *Hadeeths*, such as this *Hadeeth*. When asked by the Jews about the angel who descended to him with Divine Revelation, Prophet Muhammad (ﷺ) said,

" فَإِنَّ وَلِيِّيَ جِبْرِيلُ عَلَيْهِ السَّلَامُ وَلَمْ يَبْعَثِ اللَّهُ نَبِيًّا قَطُّ إِلاَّ وَهُوَ وَلِيُّهُ " قَالُوا: فَعِنْدَهَا نُفَارِقُكَ لَوْ كَانَ وَلِيُّكَ سِوَاهُ مِنَ الْمَلاَئِكَةِ لَتَابَعْنَاكَ وَصَدَّقْنَاكَ قَالَ: " فَمَا يَمْنَعُكُمْ مِنْ أَنْ تُصَدِّقُوهُ " قَالُوا: إِنَّهُ عَدُوُّنَا

---

[15] [*Ayah* (plural: *Ayat*): Literally, '*Ayah*', means, 'Sentence'; with regards to *Quran*, an *Ayah* is a Quranic Sentence; sometimes, *Ayat* are less accurately called 'verses'.]

"Surely, my Wali (the angel who descends to me with revelation) is Jibreel (Gabriel), peace be upon him, and Allah has never sent a prophet but with Jibreel as his Wali." The Jews said, "This is when we part with you. Had your *Wali* been another angel, we would have followed you and believed in you." The Prophet (ﷺ) asked them, *"What prevents you from believing in him (Angel Jibril)?"* They said, "He is our enemy." (A *Sahih Hadeeth*; *al-Musnad*[16] [2384])

Seventh: Human Messengers convey *Tau'heed*, i.e., Allah's Islamic Monotheism, establish practices of worship, permissible dealings and good conduct; they also deliver Allah's Promises and Warnings.

Allah (ﷻ) said,

﴿ وَمَا نُرْسِلُ ٱلْمُرْسَلِينَ إِلَّا مُبَشِّرِينَ وَمُنذِرِينَ ۖ فَمَنْ ءَامَنَ وَأَصْلَحَ فَلَا خَوْفٌ عَلَيْهِمْ وَلَا هُمْ يَحْزَنُونَ ۝ وَٱلَّذِينَ كَذَّبُوا۟ بِـَٔايَـٰتِنَا يَمَسُّهُمُ ٱلْعَذَابُ بِمَا كَانُوا۟ يَفْسُقُونَ ۝ ﴾

{*And We send not the Messengers but as Givers of glad tidings and as Warners. So whosoever believes and does righteous good deeds, upon such shall come no fear, nor shall they grieve. But those who reject Our Ayât (proofs, evidences, signs, revelations, etc.), the torment will touch them for their disbelief.*} (6:48-49)

Allah (ﷻ) also said,

---

[16] [Shaikh Ahmad Shakir (1309-1377AH/1892-1958), a major contemporary scholar of *Hadeeth*, graded this *Hadeeth* as *Sahih* (*Umdatu at-Tafsir* [1/140]).
Al-Musnad: Imam Ahmad Ibn `Hanbal (164-241AH/780-855), one of the major Muslim Scholars, collected, *al-Musnad*, which contains tens of thousands of *Hadeeth* narrations; *Al-Musnad* is a major source of *Hadeeth*.]

Muhammad's Role in Islam

﴿ وَإِلَىٰ مَدْيَنَ أَخَاهُمْ شُعَيْبًا ۚ قَالَ يَـٰقَوْمِ ٱعْبُدُوا۟ ٱللَّهَ مَا لَكُم مِّنْ إِلَـٰهٍ غَيْرُهُۥ ۖ وَلَا تَنقُصُوا۟ ٱلْمِكْيَالَ وَٱلْمِيزَانَ ۚ إِنِّىٓ أَرَىٰكُم بِخَيْرٍ وَإِنِّىٓ أَخَافُ عَلَيْكُمْ عَذَابَ يَوْمٍ مُّحِيطٍ ۝ وَيَـٰقَوْمِ أَوْفُوا۟ ٱلْمِكْيَالَ وَٱلْمِيزَانَ بِٱلْقِسْطِ ۖ وَلَا تَبْخَسُوا۟ ٱلنَّاسَ أَشْيَآءَهُمْ وَلَا تَعْثَوْا۟ فِى ٱلْأَرْضِ مُفْسِدِينَ ۝ بَقِيَّتُ ٱللَّهِ خَيْرٌ لَّكُمْ إِن كُنتُم مُّؤْمِنِينَ ۚ وَمَآ أَنَا۠ عَلَيْكُم بِحَفِيظٍ ۝ ﴾

{*And to the Madyan* (Midian) *people* (We sent) *their brother Shu'aib. He said: "O, My People! Worship Allâh, you have no other ilâh* ('god') *but Him, and give not short measure or weight. I see you in prosperity and verily, I fear for you the torment of a Day encompassing. And, O, My People! Give full measure and weight in justice and reduce not the things that are due to the people, and do not commit mischief in the land, causing corruption. That which is left by Allâh for you* (after giving the rights of the people) *is better for you, if you are believers. And I am not a guardian over you.*} (11:84-86)

Muhammad (ﷺ), the Messenger of Allah, said,

" وَلاَ شَخْصَ أَحَبُّ إِلَيْهِ الْعُذْرُ مِنَ اللَّهِ مِنْ أَجْلِ ذَلِكَ بَعَثَ اللَّهُ الْمُرْسَلِينَ مُبَشِّرِينَ وَمُنْذِرِينَ "

"*No one likes `Udhr* (i.e., 'to provide a way for the people to repent so that He accept their apologies') *more than Allah. This is why Allah sent the Messengers as Bringers of glad tidings and as Warners.*" (*Muslim* [2755])

Eighth: Allah (ﷻ) sent a prophet to every nation that existed.

Allah (ﷻ) said,

$$\text{﴿ وَإِن مِّنْ أُمَّةٍ إِلَّا خَلَا فِيهَا نَذِيرٌ ۝ ﴾}$$

{And there never was a nation but a Warner (prophet) *had passed among them*} (35:24).

Allah (ﷻ) also said,

$$\text{﴿ وَكَمْ أَرْسَلْنَا مِن نَّبِيٍّ فِي الْأَوَّلِينَ ۝ ﴾}$$

{And how many a prophet have We sent amongst the men of old} (43:6).

Allah (ﷻ) also said,

$$\text{﴿ وَلَقَدْ أَرْسَلْنَا رُسُلًا مِّن قَبْلِكَ مِنْهُم مَّن قَصَصْنَا عَلَيْكَ وَمِنْهُم مَّن لَّمْ نَقْصُصْ عَلَيْكَ ﴾}$$

{*And, indeed We have sent messengers before you* (O, Muhammad ﷺ), *of some of them We have related to you their story and of some We have not related to you their story*} (40:78).

In the *Quran*, Allah (ﷻ) summarized the Message He sent every prophet with:

$$\text{﴿ وَلَقَدْ بَعَثْنَا فِي كُلِّ أُمَّةٍ رَّسُولًا أَنِ اعْبُدُوا اللَّهَ وَاجْتَنِبُوا الطَّاغُوتَ ﴾}$$

{*And verily, We have sent among every Ummah* (community; nation) *a messenger* (proclaiming): "Worship Allâh (Alone), *and avoid* (or keep away from) *Tâghût* (all false deities [do not worship *Tâghût* besides Allâh])"} (16:36).

Muhammad's Role in Islam

Ninth: Allah (ﷻ) sent down Divine Books to His Messengers and revealed Prophetic *Sunnah* Traditions (Law) to them.

Allah (ﷻ) said,

﴿ نَزَّلَ عَلَيْكَ ٱلْكِتَٰبَ بِٱلْحَقِّ مُصَدِّقًا لِّمَا بَيْنَ يَدَيْهِ وَأَنزَلَ ٱلتَّوْرَىٰةَ وَٱلْإِنجِيلَ ۝ ﴾

{*It is He* (Allâh) *Who has sent down the Book* (the *Qur'ân*) *to you* (O, Muhammad ﷺ) *with truth, confirming what came before it. And He sent down the Taurât* (original *Torah* of Moses ﷺ) *and the Injîl* (original *Gospel* of Jesus ﷺ).} (3:3)

Allah (ﷻ) also said,

﴿ لِكُلٍّ جَعَلْنَا مِنكُمْ شِرْعَةً وَمِنْهَاجًا ﴾

{*To each among you, We have prescribed a law and a clear way*} (5:48).

Tenth: Allah (ﷻ) mentioned twenty-five of His Messengers in the *Quran*, five of whom had the strongest of will.

Allah (ﷻ) said,

﴿ وَإِذْ أَخَذْنَا مِنَ ٱلنَّبِيِّۦنَ مِيثَٰقَهُمْ وَمِنكَ وَمِن نُّوحٍ وَإِبْرَٰهِيمَ وَمُوسَىٰ وَعِيسَى ٱبْنِ مَرْيَمَ ۖ وَأَخَذْنَا مِنْهُم مِّيثَٰقًا غَلِيظًا ۝ ﴾

{*And* (remember) *when We took from the Prophets their covenant, and from you* (O, Muhammad ﷺ), *and from Nûh* (Noah ﷺ), *Ibrâhîm* (Abraham ﷺ), *Mûsâ* (Moses ﷺ), *and 'Îsâ* (Jesus ﷺ) *son of Maryam* (Mary). *We took from them a strong covenant.*} (33:7)

Allah (ﷻ) commanded Prophet Muhammad (ﷺ) to emulate the patience observed by the strong willed Messengers before him,

$$\left\{ فَٱصْبِرْ كَمَا صَبَرَ أُو۟لُوا۟ ٱلْعَزْمِ مِنَ ٱلرُّسُلِ \right\}$$

{*Therefore be patient* (O, Muhammad ﷺ) *as did the Messengers of strong will*} (46:35).

Eleventh: Muhammad (ﷺ) is Allah's Final and Last Messenger and Prophet.

Allah (ﷻ) said,

$$\left\{ مَّا كَانَ مُحَمَّدٌ أَبَآ أَحَدٍ مِّن رِّجَالِكُمْ وَلَٰكِن رَّسُولَ ٱللَّهِ وَخَاتَمَ ٱلنَّبِيِّـۧنَ ۗ وَكَانَ ٱللَّهُ بِكُلِّ شَىْءٍ عَلِيمًا \right\}$$

{*Muhammad* (ﷺ) *is not the father of any of your men, but he is the Messenger of Allâh and the last* (end) *of the Prophets. And Allâh is Ever All-Aware of everything.*} (33:40)

Muhammad (ﷺ), the Prophet of Allah, said,

" إِنَّ مَثَلِي وَمَثَلَ الأَنْبِيَاءِ مِنْ قَبْلِي كَمَثَلِ رَجُلٍ بَنَى بَيْتًا فَأَحْسَنَهُ وَأَجْمَلَهُ إِلاَّ مَوْضِعَ لَبِنَةٍ مِنْ زَاوِيَةٍ فَجَعَلَ النَّاسُ يَطُوفُونَ بِهِ وَيَعْجَبُونَ لَهُ وَيَقُولُونَ هَلاَّ وُضِعَتْ هَذِهِ اللَّبِنَةُ " قَالَ: " فَأَنَا اللَّبِنَةُ وَأَنَا خَاتِمُ النَّبِيِّينَ "

"*My similitude in comparison with other prophets before me is that of a man who built a nice, beautiful house, except for a place left in a corner for one brick. People go around the house and wonder at its beauty, but say, 'Would that this brick be put in its place!' I* [Muhammad (ﷺ)] *am that brick, and I am the last of the Prophets.*" (*Bukhari* [3271] and *Muslim* [4239])

He (ﷺ) also said,

Muhammad's Role in Islam

$$\text{" وَإِنَّهُ لاَ نَبِيَّ بَعْدِي "}$$

"And indeed, there will be no prophet after me" (*Bukhari* [3196] and *Muslim* [3429]).

Twelfth: The coming of Muhammad (ﷺ) was announced in the Books Allah revealed to earlier prophets and by their words.

Allah (ﷻ) said,

$$\text{﴿ وَإِنَّهُ لَفِى زُبُرِ ٱلْأَوَّلِينَ ۝ ﴾}$$

{*And verily, it* (the Qur'ân, and its revelation to Prophet Muhammad ﷺ) *is* (announced) *in the Scriptures* [i.e., the *Taurât* (Torah[17]) and the *Injeel* (Gospel[18])] *of former people*} (26:196).

Allah (ﷻ) also said,

$$\text{﴿ ٱلَّذِينَ يَتَّبِعُونَ ٱلرَّسُولَ ٱلنَّبِيَّ ٱلْأُمِّيَّ ٱلَّذِى يَجِدُونَهُۥ مَكْتُوبًا عِندَهُمْ فِى ٱلتَّوْرَىٰةِ وَٱلْإِنجِيلِ يَأْمُرُهُم بِٱلْمَعْرُوفِ وَيَنْهَىٰهُمْ عَنِ ٱلْمُنكَرِ وَيُحِلُّ لَهُمُ ٱلطَّيِّبَٰتِ وَيُحَرِّمُ عَلَيْهِمُ ٱلْخَبَٰٓئِثَ وَيَضَعُ عَنْهُمْ إِصْرَهُمْ وَٱلْأَغْلَٰلَ ٱلَّتِى كَانَتْ عَلَيْهِمْ ۚ فَٱلَّذِينَ ءَامَنُوا۟ بِهِۦ وَعَزَّرُوهُ وَنَصَرُوهُ وَٱتَّبَعُوا۟ ٱلنُّورَ ٱلَّذِىٓ أُنزِلَ مَعَهُۥٓ ۙ أُو۟لَٰٓئِكَ هُمُ ٱلْمُفْلِحُونَ ۝ ﴾}$$

{*Those who follow the Messenger, the Prophet who can neither read nor write* (Muhammad ﷺ) *whom they find written with them in the Taurât* (Torah) *and the Injeel* (Gospel), — *he commands them for al-Ma'rûf* (Islâmic Monotheism and all that Islâm has ordained);

---

[17] [*Deuteronomy* 18:18; *Isaiah* 42:1-13; *Habakkuk* 3:3-4]
[18] [*Matthew* 21:42-43; *John* 14:12-17, 26-28, 16:7-14)]

and forbids them from al-Munkar (disbelief, polytheism of all kinds, and all that Islâm has forbidden); *he allows them as lawful at-Tayyibât* (all good and lawful as regards things, deeds, beliefs, persons and foods), *and prohibits them as unlawful al-Khabâ'ith* (all evil and unlawful as regards things, deeds, beliefs, persons and foods), *he releases them from their heavy burdens* (of Allâh's Covenant with the children of Israel), *and from the fetters* (bindings) *that were upon them. So those who believe in him* (Muhammad ﷺ), *honor him, help him, and follow the light* (the Qur'ân) *which has been sent down with him, it is they who will be successful.*} (7:157)

Muhammad (ﷺ), the Prophet of Allah, said,

" أَنَا دَعْوَةُ أَبِي إِبْرَاهِيمَ وَكَانَ آخِرُ مَنْ بَشَّرَ بِي عِيسَى ابْنُ مَرْيَمَ عَلَيْهِ الصَّلَاةُ وَالسَّلَامُ "

"*I am* [the manifestation of] *the invocation* (to Allah) *of my father, Ibrahim* (Abraham ﷺ); *Jesus, peace and blessings be upon him, son of Mary, was the last* (Prophet) *to give the glad tidings of my coming*" (A Hasan Hadeeth; Silsilat al-A`hadeeth as-Sahi`ha`h[19] [1546]).

This *Hadeeth* is in reference to an *Ayah* wherein Allah (ﷺ) stated that Prophet Ibrahim (Abraham ﷺ), along with his son, Prophet Isma`eel (Ishmael ﷺ), invoked Allah (ﷺ) for the benefit of people of Makkah, by saying,

﴿ رَبَّنَا وَٱبْعَثْ فِيهِمْ رَسُولًا مِّنْهُمْ يَتْلُواْ عَلَيْهِمْ ءَايَٰتِكَ وَيُعَلِّمُهُمُ ٱلْكِتَٰبَ وَٱلْحِكْمَةَ وَيُزَكِّيهِمْ ۚ إِنَّكَ أَنتَ ٱلْعَزِيزُ ٱلْحَكِيمُ ۝ ﴾

---

[19] [This *Hadeeth* is from the *Hasan* grade, the lesser grade of authentic *Hadeeths*. *Silsilat al-A`hadeeth as-Sa`hi`hah*: Shaikh Nasir ad-Deen al-Albani, who died in 1999, wrote this and tens of other beneficial books on *Hadeeth, Fiqh* (Islamic Jurisprudence) and other Islamic topics. He excelled in the knowledge of *Hadeeth* in particular, especially criticism and scientific analysis of *Hadeeth* texts and chains of narrators found in *Hadeeth* Collections.]

{*"Our Lord; send among them a messenger of their own, who shall recite unto them Your Ayat and instruct them in the Book* (this Qur'ân) *and al-`Hikmah* (knowledge of Islâmic laws; wisdom; Prophethood), *and purify them. Verily, You are the All-Mighty, All-Wise."*} (2:129)

Indeed, Allah (ﷻ) answered the invocation of Prophet Ibrahim (Abraham ﷺ) and his son, Prophet Isma`eel (Ishmael ﷺ), by sending Muhammad (ﷺ), His Last and Final Prophet and Messenger, a native of Makkah.

In the *Quran*, Allah (ﷻ) also stated that Prophet `Esa (Jesus ﷺ), delivered this good news to the Children of Israel,

﴿ وَإِذْ قَالَ عِيسَى ٱبْنُ مَرْيَمَ يَٰبَنِىٓ إِسْرَٰٓءِيلَ إِنِّى رَسُولُ ٱللَّهِ إِلَيْكُم مُّصَدِّقًا لِّمَا بَيْنَ يَدَىَّ مِنَ ٱلتَّوْرَىٰةِ وَمُبَشِّرًۢا بِرَسُولٍ يَأْتِى مِنۢ بَعْدِى ٱسْمُهُۥٓ أَحْمَدُ ۖ فَلَمَّا جَآءَهُم بِٱلْبَيِّنَٰتِ قَالُوا۟ هَٰذَا سِحْرٌ مُّبِينٌ ۝ ﴾

{*And* (remember; mention) *when 'Îsâ* (Jesus), *son of Maryam* (Mary), *said: "O, Children of Israel! I am the Messenger of Allâh unto you, confirming the Taurât* [(Torah) which came] *before me, and giving glad tidings of a messenger to come after me, whose name shall be Ahmad* (Prophet Muhammad ﷺ). *But when he* (Ahmad, i.e., Muhammad ﷺ) *came to them with clear proofs, they said: "This is plain magic."*} (61:6)

Ahmad is one of the names of Prophet Muhammad (ﷺ); literally, it means, 'one who praises Allah more than others do.'

Thirteenth: Muhammad's Message is universal.

Allah (ﷺ) said,

﴿ قُلْ يَٰٓأَيُّهَا ٱلنَّاسُ إِنِّى رَسُولُ ٱللَّهِ إِلَيْكُمْ جَمِيعًا ٱلَّذِى لَهُۥ مُلْكُ ٱلسَّمَٰوَٰتِ وَٱلْأَرْضِ ۖ لَآ إِلَٰهَ إِلَّا هُوَ يُحْىِۦ وَيُمِيتُ ۖ فَـَٔامِنُوا۟ بِٱللَّهِ وَرَسُولِهِ ٱلنَّبِىِّ ٱلْأُمِّىِّ ٱلَّذِى يُؤْمِنُ بِٱللَّهِ وَكَلِمَٰتِهِۦ وَٱتَّبِعُوهُ لَعَلَّكُمْ تَهْتَدُونَ ۝ ﴾

{*Say* (O, Muhammad ﷺ): *"O Mankind! Verily, I am sent to you all as the Messenger of Allâh — to Whom belongs the dominion of the heavens and the earth. Lâ ilâha illa Huwa* (none has the right to be worshipped but He). *It is He Who gives life and causes death. So believe in Allâh and His Messenger* (Muhammad ﷺ), *the Prophet who can neither read nor write* (i.e., Muhammad ﷺ), *who believes in Allâh and His Words*[20], *and follow him so that you may be guided."*} (7:158)

In the *Quran*, Allah (ﷺ) mentioned some of His Favors on His creation,

﴿ تَبَارَكَ ٱلَّذِى نَزَّلَ ٱلْفُرْقَانَ عَلَىٰ عَبْدِهِۦ لِيَكُونَ لِلْعَٰلَمِينَ نَذِيرًا ۝ ﴾

{*Blessed be He Who sent down the Furqan* (criterion of right and wrong, i.e., this *Qur'ân*) *to His slave* (Muhammad ﷺ) *that he may be a Warner to the 'Âlamîn* (mankind and *Jinn*)} (25:1).

---

[20] [**Allâh's Words**: The *Qur'ân*, the *Taurât* (Torah), the *Injeel* (Gospel), and all other Divine Books He revealed to His Messengers; also Allâh's Word: "Be!" — and he was, i.e. 'Îsâ (Jesus) son of Maryam (Mary).]

Muhammad's Role in Islam

Fourteenth: Muhammad (ﷺ) came to testify to the truth of Allah's Messengers who came before him, resurrect a part of their law and purify their image from the distortions and slander that were added to their legacies.

The distortions include the terrible stories in the *Two Testaments* that accuse ancient prophets of murder, deceit, incest and outright polytheism. Allah (ﷻ) said,

$$﴿ بَلْ جَاءَ بِالْحَقِّ وَصَدَّقَ الْمُرْسَلِينَ ﴾$$

{*Nay! He* (Muhammad ﷺ) *has come with the truth* (Allâh's Islâmic Monotheism and this *Qur'ân*) *and he confirms the Messengers* (before him who brought Allâh's Islâmic Monotheism).} (37:37)

Among the truth that Prophet Muhammad (ﷺ) was sent with is this Quranic Sentence that defends Prophet Sulaiman's (Solomon ﷺ) sincerity of faith,

$$﴿ وَمَا كَفَرَ سُلَيْمَانُ وَلَٰكِنَّ الشَّيَاطِينَ كَفَرُوا ﴾$$

{*Sulaimân* (Prophet Solomon ﷺ) *did not disbelieve*[21], *but the Shayâtîn* (devils) *disbelieved*} (2:102).

Prophet Muhammad (ﷺ) believed in the *original* copies of the *Taurah* (Torah), *Zabur* (Psalms) and *Injeel* (Gospel); he described *Surat al-Fati`hah*, the first chapter in the *Quran*, as being,

" ... سُورَةً لَمْ يَنْزِلْ فِي التَّوْرَاةِ وَلاَ فِي الإِنْجِيلِ وَلاَ فِي الزَّبُورِ وَلاَ فِي الْقُرْآنِ مِثْلُهَا "

---

[21] [as claimed in *1 Kings* 11:1-13]

"[Al-Fati`hah:] A Surah (chapter) the like of which was never before revealed in the at-Taurah (Torah), al-Injil (Gospel), az-Zabur (Psalms) or al-Quran" (A Sahih Hadeeth; Sahih at-Tirmidhi [2875]).

Prophet Muhammad (ﷺ) resurrected the law of stoning adulterers that Allah (ﷻ) revealed to Prophet Musa (Moses ﷺ) in the *Torah*. When the Jews of Madinah asked him (ﷺ) to rule in the case of a Jewish man and a Jewess who committed adultery, he (ﷺ) ruled by the *Torah* between them, then said,

" اللَّهُمَّ إِنِّي أَوَّلُ مَنْ أَحْيَا أَمْرَكَ إِذْ أَمَاتُوهُ "

"O, Allah! I am the first to resurrect Your Commandment, after they (Jews and Christians) *had killed it."* (Muslim [3212])

Fifteenth: Muhammad (ﷺ) came to re-establish the same Message of *Tau`heed*, Allah's Islamic Monotheism, that Allah (ﷻ) revealed to every prophet and messenger He sent before him.

Allah (ﷻ) said,

﴿ وَمَآ أَرْسَلْنَا مِن قَبْلِكَ مِن رَّسُولٍ إِلَّا نُوحِىٓ إِلَيْهِ أَنَّهُۥ لَآ إِلَٰهَ إِلَّآ أَنَا۠ فَٱعْبُدُونِ ﴾

{*And We did not send any messenger before you* (O, Muhammad ﷺ) *but We revealed to him* (saying): *Lâ ilâha illa ana* [none has the right to be worshipped but I (Allâh)], *so worship Me* (Alone and none else)"} (21:25).

For instance, Allah (ﷻ) said,

﴿ لَقَدْ أَرْسَلْنَا نُوحًا إِلَىٰ قَوْمِهِۦ فَقَالَ يَٰقَوْمِ ٱعْبُدُوا۟ ٱللَّهَ مَا لَكُم مِّنْ إِلَٰهٍ غَيْرُهُۥٓ إِنِّىٓ أَخَافُ عَلَيْكُمْ عَذَابَ يَوْمٍ عَظِيمٍ ﴾

{*Indeed, We sent Nûh* (Noah ﷺ) *to his people and he said: "O, My People! Worship Allâh! You have no other Ilâh ('God') but Him. (Lâ ilâha illallâh: none has the right to be worshipped but Allâh.) Certainly, I fear for you the torment of a Great Day!"*} (7:59)

Muhammad (ﷺ), the Prophet of Allah, said,

" أَنَا أَوْلَى النَّاسِ بِعِيسَى ابْنِ مَرْيَمَ فِي الدُّنْيَا وَالآخِرَةِ وَالأَنْبِيَاءُ إِخْوَةٌ لِعَلَّاتٍ أُمَّهَاتُهُمْ شَتَّى وَدِينُهُمْ وَاحِدٌ "

"Both in this world and in the Hereafter, I am the nearest of all the people to Jesus, son of Mary. The prophets are paternal brothers: their mothers are different, but their religion is one." (Bukhari [3187] and *Muslim* [4360])

The *Old Testament* attests to the fact that every prophet whom Allah sent was sent with the Islamic Monotheism, "**4.** Hear, O Israel: The Lord our God is one Lord. **5.** And thou shalt love the Lord thy God with all thine heart, and with all thy soul, and with all thy might." (*Deuteronomy* 6:4-5)

The *New Testament* also attests to the fact that Prophet 'Esa (Jesus), peace be upon him, was sent with the Message of Islamic Monotheism, "**29.** And Jesus answered. ... The first of all the commandments is, Hear, O Israel; The Lord our God is one Lord. **30.** And thou shalt love the Lord thy God with all thy heart, and with all thy soul, and with all thy mind, and with all thy strength: this is the first commandment." (*Mark* 12:29-30)

Prophet Muhammad (ﷺ) invited mankind to the same Islamic Monotheism preached by every prophet sent by Allah (ﷻ),

" وَخَيْرُ مَا قُلْتُ أَنَا وَالنَّبِيُّونَ مِنْ قَبْلِي لَا إِلَهَ إِلَّا اللَّهُ وَحْدَهُ لَا شَرِيكَ لَهُ "

"The best statement that I and the prophets before me ever made is, 'La ilaha illa-llahu wa`hdahu la shareeka lah (There is no Ilah

['God'] except Allah, Alone, without partners)'" (A *Hasan Hadeeth*; *Sahih at-Tirmidhi* [3585]).

He (ﷺ) also said,

" ثَلَاثٌ مَنْ كُنَّ فِيهِ وَجَدَ حَلَاوَةَ الْإِيمَانِ أَنْ يَكُونَ اللَّهُ وَرَسُولُهُ أَحَبَّ إِلَيْهِ مِمَّا سِوَاهُمَا وَأَنْ يُحِبَّ الْمَرْءَ لَا يُحِبُّهُ إِلَّا لِلَّهِ وَأَنْ يَكْرَهَ أَنْ يَعُودَ فِي الْكُفْرِ كَمَا يَكْرَهُ أَنْ يُقْذَفَ فِي النَّارِ "

"Whoever possesses the following three qualities will have (feel; taste) *the sweetness* (delight) *of faith: The one to whom Allah and His Messenger become dearer than anything and anyone else; Who loves a person and he loves him only for Allah's Sake; Who hates to revert to Atheism* (disbelief) *as he hates to be thrown into the fire"* (*Bukhari* [15] and *Muslim* [60]).

Sixteenth: The *Quran* praises Prophet Muhammad's standard of character.

Allah (ﷻ) said,

﴿ وَإِنَّكَ لَعَلَىٰ خُلُقٍ عَظِيمٍ ۝ ﴾

{*And verily, you* (O, Muhammad ﷺ) *are on an exalted* (standard of) *character*} (68:4).

The Prophet's companions (رضي الله عنهم) also described him (ﷺ) the same as Allah (ﷻ) has described him.

1. Anas Ibn Malik (10BH [22] -93AH [23] /613-711), who served the Prophet (ﷺ) for ten years in Madinah, until the Prophet (ﷺ) died,

---

[22] [BH: Before the Prophet's *Hijrah*, meaning, the Prophet's migration from Makkah to Madinah in the year 623 CE]

[23] [AH: After the Prophet's *Hijrah*]

said, "The Prophet (ﷺ) was the best of all people in character" (*Bukhari* [5735] and *Muslim* [4003]).
2. Anas (؆) also said, "I served the Prophet (ﷺ) for ten years, and he never said to me, 'Uf' (a word that indicates impatience) and never blamed me by saying, 'Why did you do so,' or, 'Why didn't you do so?'" (*Bukhari* [5578] and *Muslim* [4269])
3. Aishah (6BH-57AH/617-676) (؆[24]), the Prophet's wife, said, "The Messenger of Allah (ﷺ) never struck anything with his hand, neither a woman, nor a servant" (*Muslim* [4296]).
4. When asked about the mannerism of Allah's Prophet with his family, Aishah (؆) said, "He (ﷺ) neither talked in an insulting manner, nor did he ever intentionally speak evil, nor was he a noisemaker in marketplaces. He (ﷺ) did not return the evil deed with the same, but used to forgive and pardon." (A *Hasan Sahih*[25] *Hadeeth*; *Sahih at-Tirmidhi* [2016])

Seventeenth: The *Quran* asserts Prophet Muhammad's compassionate eagerness to benefit mankind.

Allah (ﷻ) said,

﴿ لَقَدْ جَآءَكُمْ رَسُولٌ مِّنْ أَنفُسِكُمْ عَزِيزٌ عَلَيْهِ مَا عَنِتُّمْ حَرِيصٌ عَلَيْكُم بِٱلْمُؤْمِنِينَ رَءُوفٌ رَّحِيمٌ ۝ ﴾

{*Verily, there has come unto you a Messenger* (Muhammad ﷺ) *from among yourselves* (whom you know well). *It grieves him that you*

---

[24] [؆, or, 'Radhiya-llahu `anha': This statement means, 'May Allah be pleased with her'; it is recited for the benefit of the Prophet's individual female companions.]

[25] [*Hasan Sahih*: A unique terminology of *Hadeeth* used by Imam at-Tirmidhi to describe a *Hadeeth* narration that is between the *Hasan* and *Sahih* grades in strength; it may also refer to a *Hadeeth* narration reported from multiple chains of narrators, one from the grade *Hasan* and another from the grade *Sahih*.]

should receive any injury or difficulty. He (Muhammad ﷺ) *is anxious over you*[26]*; for the believers* (he is) *full of pity, kind, and merciful.*} (9:128)

Allah (ﷻ) also comforted His Prophet (ﷺ), who felt grief because his people did not believe in him, reminding him not to allow grief to overwhelm him,

﴿ فَلَعَلَّكَ بَٰخِعٌ نَّفْسَكَ عَلَىٰٓ ءَاثَٰرِهِمْ إِن لَّمْ يُؤْمِنُوا۟ بِهَٰذَا ٱلْحَدِيثِ أَسَفًا ۝ ﴾

{*Fa-la`allaka bakhi`un* (i.e., 'do not kill yourself, O, Muhammad' [this is a figure of speech]) *in grief, over their footsteps* (for their turning away from you), *because they believe not in this narration* (the *Qur'ân*)} (18:6).

Eighteenth: Prophet Muhammad (ﷺ) received the *Quran* from Allah (ﷻ) testifying to the truth contained within Books Allah (ﷻ) revealed to earlier prophets and overruling them with regards to the Law.

Allah (ﷻ) said,

﴿ وَأَنزَلْنَآ إِلَيْكَ ٱلْكِتَٰبَ بِٱلْحَقِّ مُصَدِّقًا لِّمَا بَيْنَ يَدَيْهِ مِنَ ٱلْكِتَٰبِ وَمُهَيْمِنًا عَلَيْهِ ۖ فَٱحْكُم بَيْنَهُم بِمَآ أَنزَلَ ٱللَّهُ ۖ وَلَا تَتَّبِعْ أَهْوَآءَهُمْ عَمَّا جَآءَكَ مِنَ ٱلْحَقِّ ﴾

{*And We have sent down to you* (O, Muhammad ﷺ) *the Book* (this *Qur'ân*) *in truth, confirming the Scripture that came before it and Mohayminan* (trustworthy in highness and a witness) *over it* (old Scriptures). *So judge* (you, O, Muhammad ﷺ) *among them by what*

---

[26] [i.e., to be rightly guided, to repent to Allah and to beg Him to pardon and forgive your sins in order that you may enter Paradise and be saved from punishment of the Hellfire]

Muhammad's Role in Islam

Allâh has revealed, and follow not their vain desires, diverging away from the truth that has come to you.} (5:48)

Nineteenth: The *Quran* was not the only revelation sent from Allah (ﷻ) to Prophet Muhammad (ﷺ); Muhammad's Prophetic *Sunnah* is also Divine Revelation.

Allah (ﷻ) said in the *Quran*,

﴿ لَا تُحَرِّكْ بِهِ لِسَانَكَ لِتَعْجَلَ بِهِ ۞ إِنَّ عَلَيْنَا جَمْعَهُ وَقُرْآنَهُ ۞ فَإِذَا قَرَأْنَاهُ فَاتَّبِعْ قُرْآنَهُ ۞ ثُمَّ إِنَّ عَلَيْنَا بَيَانَهُ ۞ ﴾

{*Move not your tongue concerning it* (the Qur'ân, O, Muhammad ﷺ) *to make haste therewith. It is for Us to collect it* ('in your heart, O, Muhammad ﷺ[27]') *and to give you* (O, Muhammad ﷺ) *its Qur'ân* ('the ability to recite the Qur'ân [28]'). *And when We have recited it to you* (O, Muhammad ﷺ through Our Angel Jibrîl), *then follow its Qur'ân* (the Qur'ân's recitation). *Then it is for Us* (Allâh) *to make clear its Bayan* (explanation; meaning; implication).} (75:16-19)

In his *Hadeeth*, Muhammad (ﷺ), Allah's Prophet, explained Ayat 75:16-19, by saying,

" أَلاَ إِنِّي أُوتِيتُ الْقُرْآنَ وَمِثْلَهُ مَعَهُ "

"*I was given the Quran and its equal with it* (i.e., the *Sunnah*)" (A Sahih Hadeeth; Al-Hadeethu `Hujjatun bi-Nafsihi[29] [21]).

---

[27] [Ibn Kathir, Isam`eel Ibn `Amr. *Tafsir Ibn Kathir* (Vol. 4, Pg., 578).]

[28] [Ibid.]

[29] [Albani, Muhammad Nasir ad-Deen. *Al-Hadeethu `Hujjatun bi-Nafsihi fi-l-A`hkami wa-l-`Aqa-id* (The *Hadeeth* is Proof Itself in Matters of Law and Creed) (Pg. 26-27).

Continue on next page…

Introduction to: Muhammad (ﷺ), The Prophet of Mercy

The *Quran* declared that Muhammad's Prophetic Tradition, is also a revelation from Allah (ﷻ),

﴿ وَمَا يَنطِقُ عَنِ ٱلْهَوَىٰ ۝ إِنْ هُوَ إِلَّا وَحْيٌ يُوحَىٰ ۝ ﴾

{*Wa-ma yantiqu `ani-l-hawa, in huwa illa wa`hyun yu`ha* (He, Muhammad ﷺ, does not speak of his own desire, it is only a revelation revealed)} (53:3-4).

Prophet Muhammad (ﷺ) did not only speak, or '*Nataqa* (in the present tense: *Yantiqu*)' the *Quran*, he also spoke the *Sunnah*. Abdullah Ibn `Amr Ibn al-`Aas (ﷺ) used to write everything the Prophet (ﷺ) said, meaning, his *Hadeeth* or religious statements. Muslims from the tribe of Quraish –the Prophet's tribe- criticized Abdullah for doing this, claiming that sometimes the Prophet (ﷺ) might say things in anger. Abdullah Ibn `Amr asked the Prophet (ﷺ) about it, and he (ﷺ) said, while pointing to his mouth,

" اكْتُبْ فَوَالَّذِي نَفْسِي بِيَدِهِ مَا يَخْرُجُ مِنْهُ إِلاَّ حَقٌّ "

"*Rather, write! For by He* (Allah) *in Whose Hand is my soul, nothing save Truth comes out of it.*" (A *Sahih Hadeeth*; *Sahih Sunan Abi Dawud*[30] [3646])

Continued from previous page...
Allah blessed me –this author- to translate this book into English for, Dar at-Turath al-Islami.]

[30] [*Sunan Abi Dawud*: Imam Abu Dawud as-Sujustani (202-275AH/825-898) collected the *Sunan* (pl. for *Sunnah*) known by his name; *Sunan Abi Dawud* is one of the six major Collections of *Hadeeth*.
Sahih Sunan Abi Dawud, by Shaikh Nasir ad-Deen al-Albani, lists *Sahih* (authentic) *Hadeeths* found in, *Sunan Abi Dawud*; al-Albani's *Dha`eef Sunan Abi Dawud* contains *Dha`eef* (weak) *Hadeeth* narrations found in, *Sunan Abi Dawud*.]

Twentieth: In the *Quran*, Allah (ﷻ) explained why He made a promise to teach Prophet Muhammad (ﷺ) the *Quran* in addition to its *Bayan* (explanation).

Allah (ﷻ) said,

﴿ وَأَنزَلْنَآ إِلَيْكَ ٱلذِّكْرَ لِتُبَيِّنَ لِلنَّاسِ مَا نُزِّلَ إِلَيْهِمْ وَلَعَلَّهُمْ يَتَفَكَّرُونَ ۝ ﴾

{*And We have also sent down unto you* (O, Muhammad ﷺ) *the Dhikr* (the Qur'ân), *that you may Tubayyina* (give the *Bayan*, or explain clearly) *to men what is sent down to them, and that they may give thought*} (16:44).

Allah (ﷻ) also said,

﴿ وَمَآ أَنزَلْنَا عَلَيْكَ ٱلْكِتَٰبَ إِلَّا لِتُبَيِّنَ لَهُمُ ٱلَّذِى ٱخْتَلَفُوا۟ فِيهِ ۙ وَهُدًى وَرَحْمَةً لِّقَوْمٍ يُؤْمِنُونَ ۝ ﴾

{*And We have not sent down the Book* (the Qur'ân) *to you* (O, Muhammad ﷺ), *except that you may Tubayyina* (explain clearly) *unto them those things in which they differ, and* (as) *a guidance and a mercy for a folk who believe*} (16:64).

Twenty-First: The *Quran* and Prophetic *Sunnah* explain the Pillars of *Eman*, meaning, the Islamic Faith.

Allah (ﷻ) said,

﴿ يَٰٓأَيُّهَا ٱلَّذِينَ ءَامَنُوٓا۟ ءَامِنُوا۟ بِٱللَّهِ وَرَسُولِهِ وَٱلْكِتَٰبِ ٱلَّذِى نَزَّلَ عَلَىٰ رَسُولِهِ وَٱلْكِتَٰبِ ٱلَّذِىٓ أَنزَلَ مِن قَبْلُ ۚ وَمَن يَكْفُرْ بِٱللَّهِ وَمَلَٰٓئِكَتِهِ وَكُتُبِهِ وَرُسُلِهِ وَٱلْيَوْمِ ٱلْءَاخِرِ فَقَدْ ضَلَّ ضَلَٰلًۢا بَعِيدًا ۝ ﴾

{O, You Who Believe! Believe in Allâh and His Messenger (Muhammad ﷺ), and the Book (the Qur'ân) which He has sent down to His Messenger, and the Scripture which He sent down to those before (him); and whosoever disbelieves in Allâh, His Angels, His Books, His Messengers, and the Last Day, then indeed he has strayed far away} (4:136).

Allah (ﷻ) also said,

﴿ إِنَّا كُلَّ شَيْءٍ خَلَقْنَاهُ بِقَدَرٍ ﴾

{Verily, We have created all things with Qadar³¹} (54:49).

In one of his *Hadeeths*, Muhammad (ﷺ), the Prophet of Allah, collected all six pillars of *Eman*, the Islamic Faith, mentioned in the *Ayat* quoted above; he (ﷺ) said that 'Eman' means,

" أَنْ تُؤْمِنَ بِاللَّهِ وَمَلَائِكَتِهِ وَكُتُبِهِ وَرُسُلِهِ وَالْيَوْمِ الْآخِرِ وَتُؤْمِنَ بِالْقَدَرِ خَيْرِهِ وَشَرِّهِ "

"To believe in Allah, His Angels, His Books, His Messengers and in the Last Day; and to believe in the al-Qadar (Predestination), *both the good and the evil it may bring"* (Muslim [9]).

Twenty-Second: The *Quran* and the Prophetic *Sunnah* explain the practical Pillars of Islam.

Allah (ﷻ) ordained *Ikhlas* (Sincerity) in worship, *Tau'heed* (Monotheism), *Salah* (Prayer), and *Zakah* (Charity), when He said,

---

[31] [*Qadar*: Divine Preordainments of all things before their creation as written in *al-Lau`h al-Mahfudh*, meaning, the Book of Decrees
Imam Muslim [4797] collected a *Hadeeth* in which Allah's Prophet (ﷺ) stated that fifty thousand years before creating the heavens and earth, Allah (ﷻ) wrote the destiny of all creation.]

Muhammad's Role in Islam

$$\left\{ \text{وَمَا أُمِرُوا إِلَّا لِيَعْبُدُوا اللَّهَ مُخْلِصِينَ لَهُ الدِّينَ حُنَفَاءَ وَيُقِيمُوا الصَّلَاةَ وَيُؤْتُوا الزَّكَاةَ وَذَٰلِكَ دِينُ الْقَيِّمَةِ} \right\}$$

{*And they were commanded not, but that they should worship Allâh, and worship none but Him Alone* (abstaining from ascribing partners to Him), *and perform As-Salât* (Iqâmat-as-Salât [establish Prayer perfectly and on time]) *and give Zakât* (obligatory Alms), *and that is the right religion*} (98:5).

Allah (ﷻ) also established the `Hajj as a pillar of Islam,

$$\left\{ \text{وَلِلَّهِ عَلَى النَّاسِ حِجُّ الْبَيْتِ مَنِ اسْتَطَاعَ إِلَيْهِ سَبِيلًا} \right\}$$

{*And `Hajj* (pilgrimage to Makkah) *to the House* (Ka`bah) *is a duty that mankind owes to Allâh, those who can afford the expenses* (for provision and residence)} (3:97).

Allah (ﷻ) also ordained the *Saum* (Fast) on Muslims,

$$\left\{ \text{يَا أَيُّهَا الَّذِينَ آمَنُوا كُتِبَ عَلَيْكُمُ الصِّيَامُ كَمَا كُتِبَ عَلَى الَّذِينَ مِن قَبْلِكُمْ لَعَلَّكُمْ تَتَّقُونَ} \right\}$$

{*O, You Who Believe! Observing as-Saum* (fasting during the days of the lunar month of *Ramadhan*) *is prescribed for you as it was prescribed for those before you, that you may become al-Muttaqûn* (the pious).} (2:183)

Muhammad (ﷺ), the Prophet of Islam, collected all five pillars of Islam mentioned in the *Ayat* quoted above, when he said,

"بُنِيَ الإِسْلَامُ عَلَى خَمْسٍ شَهَادَةِ أَنْ لَا إِلَهَ إِلَّا اللَّهُ وَأَنَّ مُحَمَّدًا رَسُولُ اللَّهِ وَإِقَامِ الصَّلَاةِ وَإِيتَاءِ الزَّكَاةِ وَالْحَجِّ وَصَوْمِ رَمَضَانَ"

Introduction to: Muhammad (ﷺ), The Prophet of Mercy

"*Islam is based on* (the following) *five* (principles): *To testify that there is no deity* (owing the right to be worshipped) *but Allah and that Muhammad is Allah's Messenger; to offer the* (compulsory) *prayers dutifully and perfectly, to pay Zakat* (obligatory charity), *to perform Hajj* (Pilgrimage to Makkah), *and to fast during* [the lunar month of] *Ramadan*" (*Bukhari* [7] and *Muslim* [21]).

Twenty-Third: Necessity of ruling by what Allah revealed.

Allah (ﷻ) said,

﴿ فَٱحْكُم بَيْنَهُم بِمَآ أَنزَلَ ٱللَّهُ وَلَا تَتَّبِعْ أَهْوَآءَهُمْ عَمَّا جَآءَكَ مِنَ ٱلْحَقِّ ﴾

{*So judge* (you, O, Muhammad ﷺ) *among them by what Allâh has revealed, and follow not their vain desires, diverging away from the truth that has come to you*} (5:48).

Allah (ﷻ) also ordered His Prophet (ﷺ) to rule in its entirety by what He, Allah (ﷻ), has revealed to him,

﴿ وَأَنِ ٱحْكُم بَيْنَهُم بِمَآ أَنزَلَ ٱللَّهُ وَلَا تَتَّبِعْ أَهْوَآءَهُمْ وَٱحْذَرْهُمْ أَن يَفْتِنُوكَ عَنۢ بَعْضِ مَآ أَنزَلَ ٱللَّهُ إِلَيْكَ ﴾

{*And so judge* (you, O, Muhammad ﷺ) *among them by what Allâh has revealed and follow not their vain desires, but beware of them lest they turn you* (O, Muhammad ﷺ) *far away from some of that which Allâh has sent down to you*} (5:49).

Twenty-Fourth: The *Quran* declares that Islam is life.

Allah (ﷻ) said,

﴿ يَـٰٓأَيُّهَا ٱلَّذِينَ ءَامَنُوا۟ ٱسْتَجِيبُوا۟ لِلَّهِ وَلِلرَّسُولِ إِذَا دَعَاكُمْ لِمَا يُحْيِيكُمْ ۖ وَٱعْلَمُوٓا۟ أَنَّ ٱللَّهَ يَحُولُ بَيْنَ ٱلْمَرْءِ وَقَلْبِهِۦ وَأَنَّهُۥٓ إِلَيْهِ تُحْشَرُونَ ﴾

{*O, You Who Believe! Answer Allâh* (by obeying Him) *and* (His) *Messenger when he* (ﷺ) *calls you to that which will give you life, and know that Allâh comes in between a person and his heart* (He ﷻ prevents an evil person from deciding anything). *And verily, to Him you shall* (all) *be gathered.*} (8:24)

Twenty-Fifth: Allah (ﷻ) completed and perfected Islam; Islam is a complete way of life that is to be taken as a whole.

Allah (ﷻ) said,

﴿ مَا كَانَ حَدِيثًا يُفْتَرَىٰ وَلَـٰكِن تَصْدِيقَ ٱلَّذِى بَيْنَ يَدَيْهِ وَتَفْصِيلَ كُلِّ شَىْءٍ وَهُدًى وَرَحْمَةً لِّقَوْمٍ يُؤْمِنُونَ ﴾

{*It* (the Qur'ân) *is not a forged statement but a confirmation of* (Allâh's existing Books) *which were before it* [Taurât (Torah), Injeel (Gospel) and other Scriptures of Allâh] *and a detailed explanation of everything and a guide and a mercy for the people who believe*} (12:111).

Allah (ﷻ) also warned against following in the footsteps of the devil, who strives hard to lead Muslims away from implementing any and all aspects of Islam,

$$\{ \text{يَا أَيُّهَا الَّذِينَ آمَنُوا ادْخُلُوا فِي السِّلْمِ كَافَّةً وَلَا تَتَّبِعُوا خُطُوَاتِ الشَّيْطَانِ إِنَّهُ لَكُمْ عَدُوٌّ مُبِينٌ} \text{﴾٢٠٨﴿}$$

{*O, You Who Believe! Enter perfectly in Islâm* (obey all the rules and regulations of the Islâmic religion) *and follow not the footsteps of Shaitân* (Satan). *Verily, he is to you a plain enemy.*} (2:208)

Imams Bukhari [43] and Muslim [5334] reported that Allah (ﷻ) revealed *Ayah* 5:3 to His Prophet (ﷺ) on a day that coincided with two Islamic festivals, the Day of *Arafah* during the `Hajj (Pilgrimage) season, and *Jumu`ah* (Friday), the weekly Islamic day of festival,

$$\{ \text{الْيَوْمَ أَكْمَلْتُ لَكُمْ دِينَكُمْ وَأَتْمَمْتُ عَلَيْكُمْ نِعْمَتِي وَرَضِيتُ لَكُمُ الْإِسْلَامَ دِينًا} \}$$

{*This day, I have perfected your religion for you, completed My Favor upon you, and have chosen for you Islâm as your religion*} (5:3).

Twenty-Sixth: Islam rejects all types of innovation in religion.

In the clearest of terms, *Ayah* 5:3 states that Allah (ﷻ) completed the religion of Islam, perfected His favor on His creation and chose Islam for them as their religion. ***Consequently, a religion that has been completed, perfected and chosen by Allah (ﷻ) cannot be altered or made better through additions or deletions.***

While rejecting every innovation in religion, Muhammad (ﷺ), the Prophet of Islam said,

"مَنْ أَحْدَثَ فِي أَمْرِنَا هَذَا مَا لَيْسَ فِيهِ فَهُوَ رَدٌّ"

"Whoever invents in this matter of ours (Islam) *what is not a part of it, then it* (the innovation) *is rejected" (Bukhari* [2499] and *Muslim* [3242]).

The Prophet of Allah (ﷺ) frequently emphasized the rejection of every *Bid`ah*, meaning, every innovation in religion; he used to repeat these words whenever he started his speeches,

" أَمَّا بَعْدُ فَإِنَّ خَيْرَ الْحَدِيثِ كِتَابُ اللَّهِ وَخَيْرُ الْهُدَى هُدَى مُحَمَّدٍ وَشَرُّ الْأُمُورِ مُحْدَثَاتُهَا وَكُلُّ بِدْعَةٍ ضَلَالَةٌ "

"Amma Ba`du* ('afterwards; here is what I want to say'), *fa-inna khaira-l-`hadeethi kitabu-llah, wa-khairu-l-huda huda Muhammad, wa-sharru-l-umuri mu`hdathatuha, wa-kullu bid`atin dhalalah. (Surely, the best speech is Allah's Book and the best guidance is the guidance of Muhammad. Verily, the worst matters are matters of innovation [in the religion, the *Bid`ah*], and every *Bid`ah* is a *Dhalalah* [sin, or heresy])." *(Muslim* [1435])

Twenty-Seventh: The *Quran* identifies Prophet Muhammad (ﷺ) as the example to follow.

Allah (ﷻ) said,

﴿ لَقَدْ كَانَ لَكُمْ فِي رَسُولِ ٱللَّهِ أُسْوَةٌ حَسَنَةٌ لِّمَن كَانَ يَرْجُواْ ٱللَّهَ وَٱلْيَوْمَ ٱلْأَخِرَ وَذَكَرَ ٱللَّهَ كَثِيرًا ﴾

{*Indeed in the Messenger of Allâh* (Muhammad ﷺ) *you have a good example to follow for him who hopes for* (the Meeting with) *Allâh and the* (the good of the) *Last Day, and remembers Allâh much*} (33:21).

Introduction to: Muhammad (ﷺ), The Prophet of Mercy

Twenty-Eighth: In the *Quran*, Allah (ﷻ) ordered Muslims to refer to Prophet Muhammad (ﷺ) for judgment if they fall into any type of dispute.

Allah (ﷻ) said,

﴿ فَإِن تَنَٰزَعْتُمْ فِى شَىْءٍ فَرُدُّوهُ إِلَى ٱللَّهِ وَٱلرَّسُولِ إِن كُنتُمْ تُؤْمِنُونَ بِٱللَّهِ وَٱلْيَوْمِ ٱلْءَاخِرِ ﴾

{(And) *if you differ in anything amongst yourselves, refer it to Allâh (the Qur'ân) and His Messenger (his Sunnah[32]), if you believe in Allâh and the Last Day*} (4:59).

Allah (ﷻ) revealed two distinct types of instructions, the *Quran* and Muhammad's *Sunnah*,

﴿ لَقَدْ مَنَّ ٱللَّهُ عَلَى ٱلْمُؤْمِنِينَ إِذْ بَعَثَ فِيهِمْ رَسُولًا مِّنْ أَنفُسِهِمْ يَتْلُواْ عَلَيْهِمْ ءَايَٰتِهِۦ وَيُزَكِّيهِمْ وَيُعَلِّمُهُمُ ٱلْكِتَٰبَ وَٱلْحِكْمَةَ وَإِن كَانُواْ مِن قَبْلُ لَفِى ضَلَٰلٍ مُّبِينٍ ﴾

{*Indeed, Allâh conferred a great favor on the believers when He sent among them a Messenger* (Muhammad ﷺ) *from among themselves, reciting unto them His Ayat* (the *Qur'ân*), *and purifying them* (from sins by their following him), *and instructing them* (in) *the Book* (the *Qur'ân*) *and al-`Hikmah* (wisdom; Muhammad's *Sunnah*, legal ways, statements, and acts of worship), *while before that they had been in manifest error*} (3:164).

---

[32] [Ibn Kathir, Isam`eel Ibn `Amr. *Tafsir Ibn Kathir* (Vol. 1, Pg., 689).]

Muhammad's Role in Islam

Twenty-Ninth: Allah (ﷻ) did not give the believers the option to choose which part of His Revelation they want to abide by.

Allah (ﷻ) said,

﴿ وَمَا كَانَ لِمُؤْمِنٍ وَلَا مُؤْمِنَةٍ إِذَا قَضَى ٱللَّهُ وَرَسُولُهُۥ أَمْرًا أَن يَكُونَ لَهُمُ ٱلْخِيَرَةُ مِنْ أَمْرِهِمْ ۗ وَمَن يَعْصِ ٱللَّهَ وَرَسُولَهُۥ فَقَدْ ضَلَّ ضَلَٰلًا مُّبِينًا ﴾

{*It is not for a believer, man or woman, when Allâh and His Messenger have decreed a matter that they should have any option in their decision. And whoever disobeys Allâh and His Messenger, he has indeed strayed into a plain error.*} (33:36)

Thirtieth: Allah (ﷻ) made earning His Love conditional upon the *Ittiba`*, the following of and obedience to His Prophet (ﷺ).

In the *Quran*, Allah (ﷻ) said,

﴿ قُلْ إِن كُنتُمْ تُحِبُّونَ ٱللَّهَ فَٱتَّبِعُونِى يُحْبِبْكُمُ ٱللَّهُ وَيَغْفِرْ لَكُمْ ذُنُوبَكُمْ ۗ وَٱللَّهُ غَفُورٌ رَّحِيمٌ ﴾

{*Say (O, Muhammad ﷺ to mankind): "If you (really) love Allâh, then follow me, Allâh will love you and forgive you your sins. And Allâh is Oft-Forgiving, Most Merciful."*} (3:31)

Introduction to: Muhammad (ﷺ), The Prophet of Mercy

Thirty-First: In the *Quran*, Allah (ﷻ) made referring to His Prophet's judgment in every dispute or difference that arises between Muslims the sign that distinguishes *Eman* (Faith).

Allah (ﷻ) said,

﴿ فَلَا وَرَبِّكَ لَا يُؤْمِنُونَ حَتَّىٰ يُحَكِّمُوكَ فِيمَا شَجَرَ بَيْنَهُمْ ثُمَّ لَا يَجِدُوا فِي أَنفُسِهِمْ حَرَجًا مِّمَّا قَضَيْتَ وَيُسَلِّمُوا تَسْلِيمًا ﴾

{But no, by your Lord, they can have no Eman (Faith), until they make you (O, Muhammad ﷺ) judge in all disputes between them, and find in themselves no resistance against your decisions, and accept (them) with full submission} (4:65).

Thirty-Second: Whoever obeys the Prophet's commandments obeys Allah Himself; whoever disobeys the Prophet's commandments disobeys Allah Himself.

Allah (ﷻ) said,

﴿ مَّن يُطِعِ ٱلرَّسُولَ فَقَدْ أَطَاعَ ٱللَّهَ ﴾

{He who obeys the Messenger (Muhammad ﷺ), has indeed obeyed Allâh} (4:80).

Allah (ﷻ) ordered the believers to fulfill the Prophet's commandments and avoid what he prohibits for them,

﴿ وَمَآ ءَاتَىٰكُمُ ٱلرَّسُولُ فَخُذُوهُ وَمَا نَهَىٰكُمْ عَنْهُ فَٱنتَهُوا۟ ﴾

{And whatsoever the Messenger (Muhammad ﷺ) gives you, take it; and whatsoever he forbids you, abstain (from it)} (59:7).

Muhammad (ﷺ), the Prophet of Allah, said,

" مَنْ أَطَاعَنِي فَقَدْ أَطَاعَ اللَّهَ وَمَنْ عَصَانِي فَقَدْ عَصَى اللَّهَ "

"He who obeys me obeys Allah, and he who disobeys me disobeys Allah" (Bukhari [6604] and Muslim [3418]).

Thirty-Third: The *Quran* gives a clear example of the consequence of defying the Prophet's *Amr*, meaning, his commandments and *Sunnah* Traditions.

Allah (ﷻ) said,

﴿ فَلْيَحْذَرِ ٱلَّذِينَ يُخَالِفُونَ عَنْ أَمْرِهِ أَن تُصِيبَهُمْ فِتْنَةٌ أَوْ يُصِيبَهُمْ عَذَابٌ أَلِيمٌ ۝ ﴾

{And let those who oppose the Messenger's (Muhammad's) *Amr* (his *Sunnah*, legal ways, orders, acts of worship, statements) *beware, lest some Fitnah* (trials in life and religion) *should befall them or a painful torment be inflicted on them*} (24:63).

Allah (ﷻ) also said,

﴿ وَأَطِيعُواْ ٱللَّهَ وَرَسُولَهُۥ وَلَا تَنَٰزَعُواْ فَتَفْشَلُواْ وَتَذْهَبَ رِيحُكُمْ ۖ وَٱصْبِرُوٓاْ ۚ إِنَّ ٱللَّهَ مَعَ ٱلصَّٰبِرِينَ ۝ ﴾

{And obey Allâh and His Messenger (Muhammad ﷺ), *and do not dispute* (with one another) *lest you lose courage and your strength departs, and be patient. Surely, Allâh is with those who are as-Sâbirûn* (the patient).} (8:46)

Thirty-Fourth: The *Quran* warns against hypocrisy manifested by rejecting referring to the Prophet (ﷺ) for judgment.

Allah (ﷻ) said,

﴿ أَلَمْ تَرَ إِلَى ٱلَّذِينَ يَزْعُمُونَ أَنَّهُمْ ءَامَنُوا۟ بِمَآ أُنزِلَ إِلَيْكَ وَمَآ أُنزِلَ مِن قَبْلِكَ يُرِيدُونَ أَن يَتَحَاكَمُوٓا۟ إِلَى ٱلطَّٰغُوتِ وَقَدْ أُمِرُوٓا۟ أَن يَكْفُرُوا۟ بِهِۦ وَيُرِيدُ ٱلشَّيْطَٰنُ أَن يُضِلَّهُمْ ضَلَٰلًۢا بَعِيدًا ۝ وَإِذَا قِيلَ لَهُمْ تَعَالَوْا۟ إِلَىٰ مَآ أَنزَلَ ٱللَّهُ وَإِلَى ٱلرَّسُولِ رَأَيْتَ ٱلْمُنَٰفِقِينَ يَصُدُّونَ عَنكَ صُدُودًا ۝ فَكَيْفَ إِذَآ أَصَٰبَتْهُم مُّصِيبَةٌۢ بِمَا قَدَّمَتْ أَيْدِيهِمْ ثُمَّ جَآءُوكَ يَحْلِفُونَ بِٱللَّهِ إِنْ أَرَدْنَآ إِلَّآ إِحْسَٰنًا وَتَوْفِيقًا ۝ أُو۟لَٰٓئِكَ ٱلَّذِينَ يَعْلَمُ ٱللَّهُ مَا فِى قُلُوبِهِمْ فَأَعْرِضْ عَنْهُمْ وَعِظْهُمْ وَقُل لَّهُمْ فِىٓ أَنفُسِهِمْ قَوْلًۢا بَلِيغًا ۝ وَمَآ أَرْسَلْنَا مِن رَّسُولٍ إِلَّا لِيُطَاعَ بِإِذْنِ ٱللَّهِ وَلَوْ أَنَّهُمْ إِذ ظَّلَمُوٓا۟ أَنفُسَهُمْ جَآءُوكَ فَٱسْتَغْفَرُوا۟ ٱللَّهَ وَٱسْتَغْفَرَ لَهُمُ ٱلرَّسُولُ لَوَجَدُوا۟ ٱللَّهَ تَوَّابًا رَّحِيمًا ۝ فَلَا وَرَبِّكَ لَا يُؤْمِنُونَ حَتَّىٰ يُحَكِّمُوكَ فِيمَا شَجَرَ بَيْنَهُمْ ثُمَّ لَا يَجِدُوا۟ فِىٓ أَنفُسِهِمْ حَرَجًۭا مِّمَّا قَضَيْتَ وَيُسَلِّمُوا۟ تَسْلِيمًا ۝ ﴾

{*Have you not seen those* (hypocrites) *who claim that they believe in that which has been sent down to you* (O, Muhammad ﷺ), *and that which was sent down before you, and they wish to go for judgment* (in their disputes) *to the Tâghût* (false judges) *while they have been ordered to reject them. But Shaitân* (Satan) *wishes to lead them far astray. And when it is said to them: "Come to what Allâh has sent down and to the Messenger* (Muhammad ﷺ)*," you* (Muhammad ﷺ) *see the hypocrites turn away from you* (Muhammad ﷺ) *with aversion. How then, when a catastrophe befalls them because of what their hands have sent forth, they come to you* swearing by Allâh, "We meant no more than goodwill and conciliation!" They (hypocrites) *are those of whom Allâh knows what is in their hearts; so turn aside from them* (do not punish them) *but admonish them, and speak to them an effective word to reach their innerselves. We sent no messenger, but to be obeyed by Allâh's Leave. If they* (hypocrites), *when they had been unjust to themselves, had come to you* (Muhammad ﷺ) *and begged Allâh's forgiveness, and the Messenger had begged forgiveness for them, indeed, they would have found Allâh All-Forgiving, Most Merciful. But no, by your Lord, they can have no Faith, until they make you* (O, Muhammad ﷺ) *judge in all disputes between them, and find in themselves no resistance against your decisions, and accept* (them) *with full submission.*} (4:60-65)

Thirty-Fifth: The *Quran* orders all Muslims to follow the faith in the method of the companions of Muhammad (ﷺ).

Allah (ﷻ) said,

﴿ فَإِنْ ءَامَنُوا۟ بِمِثْلِ مَآ ءَامَنتُم بِهِۦ فَقَدِ ٱهْتَدَوا۟ ۖ وَّإِن تَوَلَّوْا۟ فَإِنَّمَا هُمْ فِى شِقَاقٍ ۖ ﴾

{*If they believe the way you believe then they are rightly guided; but if they turn away, then they are only in opposition* (defiance; rebellion)} (2:137).

The companions of Muhammad (ﷺ) used to utter a righteous statement whenever they were called to obey Allah (ﷻ) and follow His Messenger (ﷺ); Allah (ﷻ) reported their statement in the *Quran*, when He said,

﴿ إِنَّمَا كَانَ قَوْلَ ٱلْمُؤْمِنِينَ إِذَا دُعُوٓا۟ إِلَى ٱللَّهِ وَرَسُولِهِۦ لِيَحْكُمَ بَيْنَهُمْ أَن يَقُولُوا۟ سَمِعْنَا وَأَطَعْنَا ۚ وَأُو۟لَٰٓئِكَ هُمُ ٱلْمُفْلِحُونَ ۝ ﴾

Introduction to: Muhammad (ﷺ), The Prophet of Mercy

{*The only saying of the faithful believers, when they are called to Allâh* (His Words, the *Qur'ân*) *and His Messenger* (Muhammad ﷺ), *to judge between them, is that they say: "We hear and we obey." And such are the successful* (who will live forever in Paradise).} (24:51)

'The faithful believers' mentioned in *Ayah* 24:51 is a statement of truth that first, best and foremost describes the companions of Muhammad (ﷺ). Abu Hurairah (ؓ) said, "When *Ayah* [2:284] was revealed to the Messenger of Allah (ﷺ),

﴿لِلَّهِ مَا فِى ٱلسَّمَـٰوَٰتِ وَمَا فِى ٱلْأَرْضِ ۗ وَإِن تُبْدُواْ مَا فِىٓ أَنفُسِكُمْ أَوْ تُخْفُوهُ يُحَاسِبْكُم بِهِ ٱللَّهُ ۖ فَيَغْفِرُ لِمَن يَشَآءُ وَيُعَذِّبُ مَن يَشَآءُ ۗ وَٱللَّهُ عَلَىٰ كُلِّ شَىْءٍ قَدِيرٌ﴾

{*To Allâh belongs all that is in the heavens and all that is on the earth, and whether you disclose what is in your own selves or conceal it, Allâh will call you to account for it. Then He forgives whom He wills and punishes whom He wills. And Allâh is Able to do all things*}, the companions of the Messenger of Allah (ﷺ) felt it hard and severe. They came to the Messenger of Allah (ﷺ), fell to their knees and said, 'O, Messenger of Allah! We were assigned duties that are within our ability to perform, such as prayer, fasting, *Jihad*, and charity. Then, this (the above-mentioned) *Ayah* was revealed to you, and it is beyond our power to live up to it.' The Messenger of Allah (ﷺ) said,

" أَتُرِيدُونَ أَنْ تَقُولُوا كَمَا قَالَ أَهْلُ الْكِتَابَيْنِ مِنْ قَبْلِكُمْ سَمِعْنَا وَعَصَيْنَا بَلْ قُولُوا سَمِعْنَا وَأَطَعْنَا غُفْرَانَكَ رَبَّنَا وَإِلَيْكَ الْمَصِيرُ "

'*Do you intend to say what the People of the Book* (Jews and Christians) *said before you, 'We hear and we disobey?' You should rather say, 'We hear and we obey; (we seek) Your Forgiveness, our Lord! And unto You is the return.*' They said, 'We hear and we obey; (we seek) Your Forgiveness, Our Lord! And unto You is the

Muhammad's Role in Islam

return.' When the people recited this statement, it smoothly flowed on their tongues, then Allah (ﷺ) revealed immediately afterwards,

﴿ ءَامَنَ ٱلرَّسُولُ بِمَآ أُنزِلَ إِلَيْهِ مِن رَّبِّهِۦ وَٱلْمُؤْمِنُونَ ۚ كُلٌّ ءَامَنَ بِٱللَّهِ وَمَلَـٰٓئِكَتِهِۦ وَكُتُبِهِۦ وَرُسُلِهِۦ لَا نُفَرِّقُ بَيْنَ أَحَدٍ مِّن رُّسُلِهِۦ ۚ وَقَالُوا۟ سَمِعْنَا وَأَطَعْنَا ۖ غُفْرَانَكَ رَبَّنَا وَإِلَيْكَ ٱلْمَصِيرُ ۝ ﴾

{*The Messenger* (Muhammad ﷺ) *believes in what has been sent down to him from his Lord, and* (so do) *the believers. Each one believes in Allâh, His Angels, His Books, and His Messengers.* (They say,) *"We make no distinction between one another of His Messengers"* — *and they say, "We hear, and we obey.* (We seek) *Your forgiveness, our Lord, and to You is the return* (of all)."} [2:285]. When they did that (when they said, 'We hear and we obey'), Allah (ﷺ) abrogated [*Ayah* 2:284] and revealed [2:286],

﴿ لَا يُكَلِّفُ ٱللَّهُ نَفْسًا إِلَّا وُسْعَهَا ۚ لَهَا مَا كَسَبَتْ وَعَلَيْهَا مَا ٱكْتَسَبَتْ ۗ رَبَّنَا لَا تُؤَاخِذْنَآ إِن نَّسِينَآ أَوْ أَخْطَأْنَا ﴾

{*Allâh burdens not a person beyond his scope. He gets reward for that* (good) *which he has earned, and he is punished for that* (evil) *which he has earned. "Our Lord! Punish us not if we forget or fall into error."*}; He (Allah ﷺ) said, '*Yes*[33]';

﴿ رَبَّنَا وَلَا تَحْمِلْ عَلَيْنَآ إِصْرًا كَمَا حَمَلْتَهُۥ عَلَى ٱلَّذِينَ مِن قَبْلِنَا ﴾

{*"Our Lord! Lay not on us a burden like that which You did lay on those before us* (Jews and Christians).*"*}; He (Allah ﷺ) said, '*Yes*';

---

[33] [i.e., those who state that they hear and obey and recite this and the following statements, will have their invocation accepted by Allah (ﷺ)]

[50]

$$\{ \text{رَبَّنَا وَلَا تُحَمِّلْنَا مَا لَا طَاقَةَ لَنَا بِهِ} \}$$

{"Our Lord! Put not on us a burden greater than we have strength to bear."}; He (Allah ﷻ) said, 'Yes';

$$\{ \text{وَاعْفُ عَنَّا وَاغْفِرْ لَنَا وَارْحَمْنَا أَنتَ مَوْلَىٰنَا فَانصُرْنَا عَلَى الْقَوْمِ الْكَافِرِينَ} \}$$

{"Pardon us and grant us forgiveness. Have mercy on us. You are our Maulâ (Patron, Supporter and Protector), give us victory over the disbelieving people."} [2:286]; He (Allah ﷻ) said, 'Yes.'" (Muslim [179])

Allah (ﷻ) declared that He forgave the Prophet's companions (ﷺ) on account of their faithful obedience to His Messenger (ﷺ),

$$\{ \text{لَّقَد تَّابَ اللَّهُ عَلَى النَّبِيِّ وَالْمُهَاجِرِينَ وَالْأَنصَارِ الَّذِينَ اتَّبَعُوهُ فِي سَاعَةِ الْعُسْرَةِ} \}$$

{Allâh has forgiven the Prophet, the Muhâjirûn[34] and the Ansâr[35] who followed him (Prophet Muhammad ﷺ) in the time of distress (Tabûk expedition)} (9:117).

Allah (ﷻ) promised Paradise to the *Muhajirun*, who migrated from Makkah to Madinah to escape religious persecution, the *Ansar* of Madinah, who gave refuge to the *Muhajirun*, and those who follow the path taken by the *Muhajriun* and the *Ansar*,

---

[34] [*Al-Muhajirun*: Muslims who migrated from Makkah to Madinah.]
[35] [*Al-Ansar*: Muslim Residents of Madinah who gave shelter, support and aid to the *Muhajirun*.]

Muhammad's Role in Islam

﴿ وَٱلسَّٰبِقُونَ ٱلۡأَوَّلُونَ مِنَ ٱلۡمُهَٰجِرِينَ وَٱلۡأَنصَارِ وَٱلَّذِينَ ٱتَّبَعُوهُم بِإِحۡسَٰنٖ رَّضِيَ ٱللَّهُ عَنۡهُمۡ وَرَضُواْ عَنۡهُ وَأَعَدَّ لَهُمۡ جَنَّٰتٖ تَجۡرِي تَحۡتَهَا ٱلۡأَنۡهَٰرُ خَٰلِدِينَ فِيهَآ أَبَدٗاۚ ذَٰلِكَ ٱلۡفَوۡزُ ٱلۡعَظِيمُ ﴾

{And the foremost to embrace Islâm of the Muhâjirûn and the Ansâr and also those who followed them exactly (in Faith), Allâh is well-pleased with them as they are well-pleased with Him. He has prepared for them Gardens under which rivers flow (Paradise), to dwell therein forever. That is the supreme success.} (9:100)

Allah (ﷻ) also warned Muslims against defying the way of His Prophet's companions,

﴿ وَمَن يُشَاقِقِ ٱلرَّسُولَ مِنۢ بَعۡدِ مَا تَبَيَّنَ لَهُ ٱلۡهُدَىٰ وَيَتَّبِعۡ غَيۡرَ سَبِيلِ ٱلۡمُؤۡمِنِينَ نُوَلِّهِۦ مَا تَوَلَّىٰ وَنُصۡلِهِۦ جَهَنَّمَۖ وَسَآءَتۡ مَصِيرًا ﴾

{And whoever contradicts and opposes the Messenger (Muhammad ﷺ) after the right path has been shown clearly to him, and follows other than the believers' way, We shall keep him in the path he has chosen, and burn him in Hell, what an evil destination!} (4:115)

Muhammad (ﷺ), the Prophet of Allah, reasserted the praise of his companions (ﷺ) mentioned in the *Quran*, by saying,

" خَيْرُ النَّاسِ قَرْنِي ثُمَّ الَّذِينَ يَلُونَهُمْ ثُمَّ الَّذِينَ يَلُونَهُمْ "

"The best people are my generation, then the next generation, then the next generation" (*Bukhari* [2458] and *Muslim* [4601]).

Thirty-Sixth: Allah (ﷻ) promised to protect the *Dhikr* from corruption, by protecting every letter of the *Quran* in addition to its *Bayan* (meaning; explanation; implication).

Allah (ﷻ) said,

﴿ إِنَّا نَحْنُ نَزَّلْنَا ٱلذِّكْرَ وَإِنَّا لَهُۥ لَحَٰفِظُونَ ۝ ﴾

{*Verily, We, it is We Who have sent down the Dhikr* (i.e., the *Qur'ân*) *and surely, We will guard it* (from corruption)} (15:9).

Thirty-Seventh: *Dhikr* comprises of the *Quran* and the Prophet's *Sunnah*, the *Quran's* practical *Bayan*.

Allah (ﷻ) ordered His Prophet's wives to,

﴿ وَٱذْكُرْنَ مَا يُتْلَىٰ فِى بُيُوتِكُنَّ مِنْ ءَايَٰتِ ٱللَّهِ وَٱلْحِكْمَةِ ﴾

{*And remember* (in Arabic, 'Wadh-kurna', derived from 'Dhikr') *that which is recited in your houses of the Ayat of Allâh* (Qur'ân) *and al-`Hikmah* (the *Sunnah*[36])} (33:34).

Muhammad (ﷺ), the Prophet of Allah, used to teach his wives his *Sunnah*, also described in the *Quran* as, '*Hikmah*', such as teaching them the *Bayan* (meaning) of the *Quran*. Aishah (ﺭ) said, "I asked the Messenger of Allah (ﷺ) if this *Ayah* [23:60] is about those who drink alcohol and steal (major sins in Islam),

﴿ وَٱلَّذِينَ يُؤْتُونَ مَآ ءَاتَوا۟ وَّقُلُوبُهُمْ وَجِلَةٌ أَنَّهُمْ إِلَىٰ رَبِّهِمْ رَٰجِعُونَ ۝ ﴾

---

[36] [Imam Bukhari reported the statement that, `Hikmah pertains to the Prophet's *Sunnah*, from Imam Qatadah Ibn Di`amah (60-118AH/679-736), a major scholar of *Tafsiru al-Quran*, i.e., the meaning contained in the *Quran*.]

{*And those who do what they do with their hearts full of fear, because they are sure to return to their Lord.*}"

The Prophet (ﷺ) replied,

" لاَ يَا بِنْتَ الصِّدِّيقِ وَلَكِنَّهُمُ الَّذِينَ يَصُومُونَ وَيُصَلُّونَ وَيَتَصَدَّقُونَ وَهُمْ يَخَافُونَ أَنْ لاَ يُقْبَلَ مِنْهُمْ: ﴿ أُوْلَٰٓئِكَ يُسَٰرِعُونَ فِى ٱلْخَيْرَٰتِ ﴾ "

"No, Daughter of as-Siddique[37]! They are those who fast, pray and give charity, but are afraid that these actions will not be accepted of them[38], {*It is these who hasten in the good deeds.*} [23:61]" (A Sahih Hadeeth; Sahih at-Tirmidhi [3175])

Thirty-Eighth: The *Sunnah* includes the *Quran*'s practical *Bayan* (meaning), the same *Bayan* that Allah (ﷻ) promised to teach His Prophet (ﷺ) so he could teach it to others.

Allah (ﷻ) said,

﴿ وَأَنزَلْنَآ إِلَيْكَ ٱلذِّكْرَ لِتُبَيِّنَ لِلنَّاسِ مَا نُزِّلَ إِلَيْهِمْ وَلَعَلَّهُمْ يَتَفَكَّرُونَ ۝ ﴾

{*And We have also sent down unto you* (O, Muhammad ﷺ) *the Dhikr (Qur'ân), that you may Tubayyina* (give the *Bayan*; explain clearly) *to men what is sent down to them, and that they may give thought*} (16:44).

Abdullah Ibn Mas'ud (ﷺ), Prophet Muhammad's close associate and companion, said,

---

[37] ['Daughter of the Truthful One', as Abu Bakr, Aishah's father, was called]

[38] [fearful that their sincerity may have been deficient or that their actions may not have been properly performed according to the *Sunnah*]

لَمَّا نَزَلَتْ هَذِهِ الآيَةُ: ﴿ ٱلَّذِينَ ءَامَنُوا۟ وَلَمْ يَلْبِسُوٓا۟ إِيمَـٰنَهُم بِظُلْمٍ أُو۟لَـٰٓئِكَ لَهُمُ ٱلْأَمْنُ وَهُم مُّهْتَدُونَ ۝ ﴾ شَقَّ ذَلِكَ عَلَى أَصْحَابِ النَّبِيِّ صَلَّى اللَّهُ عَلَيْهِ وَسَلَّمَ وَقَالُوا: أَيُّنَا لَمْ يَظْلِمْ نَفْسَهُ؟ فَقَالَ رَسُولُ اللَّهِ صَلَّى اللَّهُ عَلَيْهِ وَسَلَّمَ: " لَيْسَ كَمَا تَظُنُّونَ إِنَّمَا هُوَ كَمَا قَالَ لُقْمَانُ لِابْنِهِ: ﴿ يَـٰبُنَىَّ لَا تُشْرِكْ بِٱللَّهِ إِنَّ ٱلشِّرْكَ لَظُلْمٌ عَظِيمٌ ۝ ﴾ "

"When *Ayah* [6:82], {*It is those who believe* (in the Oneness of Allâh and worship none but Him Alone) *and confuse not their Belief with Dhulm* (literally means, 'wrong'), *for them* (only) *there is security and they are the guided*} was revealed, it was very hard on the companions of the Prophet (ﷺ), who said, 'Who among us has not confused his belief with wrong?' The Messenger of Allah (ﷺ), said, '*It is not what you think. Rather, it is as Luqman said to his son, {O, My Son! Join not in worship others with Allâh. Verily, joining others in worship with Allâh is a great Dhûlm* (wrong; iniquity) *indeed.*} [31:13]'" (*Bukhari* [6424] and *Muslim* [178])

The Prophet's companions took the word, *Dhulm*, literally, to mean every type of wrongdoing. However, the Prophet of Allah (ﷺ) gave them the correct *Bayan* of *Ayah* 6:82, by referring them to *Ayah* 31:13. *Ayah* 31:13 indicates that the *Dhulm* mentioned in *Ayah* 6:82 pertains to *Shirk*, joining others in worship besides Allah, not every type of wrongdoing.

Conclusion: In the *Quran*, Allah (ﷺ) asserted the significance of His Prophet's *Sunnah* in various ways and in numerous instances, as these few *Ayat* indicate, what translated means,

❋ {*Indeed in the Messenger of Allâh* (Muhammad ﷺ) *you have a good example to follow for him who hopes for* (the Meeting with) *Allâh and the Last Day, and remembers Allâh much*} (33:21);

- {(And) *if you differ in anything amongst yourselves, refer it to Allâh* (the *Qur'ân*) *and His Messenger* (his *Sunnah*), *if you believe in Allâh and in the Last Day*} (4:59);
- {*Indeed, Allâh conferred a great favor on the believers when He sent among them a Messenger* (Muhammad ﷺ) *from amongst themselves, reciting unto them His Ayat* (the *Qur'ân*), *and purifying them* (from sins by their following him), *and instructing them* (in) *the Book* (the *Qur'ân*) *and al-`Hikmah* (the *Sunnah* of the Prophet ﷺ), *while before that they had been in manifest error*} (3:164);
- {*It is not for a believer, man or woman, when Allâh and His Messenger have decreed a matter that they should have any option in their decision*} (33:36);
- {*Say* (O, Muhammad ﷺ to mankind): *"If you* (really) *love Allâh, then follow me, Allâh will love you and forgive you your sins"*} (3:31);
- {*But no, by your Lord, they can have no Faith, until they make you* (O, Muhammad ﷺ) *judge in all disputes between them, and find in themselves no resistance against your decisions, and accept* (them) *with full submission*} (4:65);
- {*He who obeys the Messenger* (Muhammad ﷺ), *has indeed obeyed Allâh*} (4:80);
- {*And whatsoever the Messenger* (Muhammad ﷺ) *gives you, take it; and whatsoever he forbids you, abstain* (from it)} (59:7);
- {*And let those who oppose the Messenger's* (Muhammad's) *Amr* (his *Sunnah*) *beware, lest some Fitnah* (trials in life and religion) *should befall them or a painful torment be inflicted on them*} (24:63);
- {*And obey Allâh and His Messenger* (Muhammad ﷺ), *and do not dispute* (with one another) *lest you lose courage and your strength departs, and be patient*} (8:46);
- {*And whoever contradicts and opposes the Messenger* (Muhammad ﷺ) *after the right path has been shown clearly to him, and follows other than the believers' way, We shall keep*

him in the path he has chosen, and burn him in Hell, what an evil destination!} (4:115);

- {*Verily, We, it is We Who have sent down the Dhikr* (the *Qur'ân*) *and surely, We will guard it* (from corruption)} (15:9);
- {*And We have also sent down unto you* (O, Muhammad ﷺ) *the Dhikr* (the *Qur'ân*), *that you may Tubayyina* (give the *Bayan*, or explain clearly) *to men what is sent down to them, and that they may give thought*} (16:44);
- {*The only saying of the faithful believers, when they are called to Allâh* (His Words, the *Qur'ân*) *and His Messenger* (Muhammad's *Sunnah*), *to judge between them, is that they say: "We hear and we obey!"*} (24:51)

Thirty-Ninth: By Allah's Permission, Prophet Muhammad (ﷺ) established the Islamic *Sharee`ah* (Law).

By Allah's Permission, Prophet Muhammad (ﷺ) established the Islamic *Sharee`ah* (Law), legislating the Islamic acts of worship, penal code, code of good conduct, outward attire, Islam's economic, social, educational, political and military systems and what is allowed or disallowed of foods, drinks, dealings and contracts.

Throughout his Prophethood, Muhammad (ﷺ), the Prophet of Allah, taught his companions (﷠) the practical pillars of Islam, such as manners of the *Salah* (Prayer), *Zakat* (Charity), *Saum* (Fast) and `*Hajj* (Pilgrimage). These are duly recorded and preserved in various *Sunnah* Collections.

Here are a few examples wherein the Prophet of Allah (ﷺ) legislates various aspects of Islam's major acts of worship.

1. The Prophet of Allah (ﷺ) asserted the significance of pronouncing the Two Testimonials, by saying,

> " مَنْ شَهِدَ أَنْ لاَ إِلَهَ إِلاَّ اللَّهُ وَحْدَهُ لاَ شَرِيكَ لَهُ وَأَنَّ مُحَمَّدًا عَبْدُهُ وَرَسُولُهُ وَأَنَّ عِيسَى عَبْدُ اللَّهِ وَرَسُولُهُ وَكَلِمَتُهُ أَلْقَاهَا إِلَى مَرْيَمَ وَرُوحٌ مِنْهُ وَالْجَنَّةُ حَقٌّ وَالنَّارُ حَقٌّ أَدْخَلَهُ اللَّهُ الْجَنَّةَ عَلَى مَا كَانَ مِنَ الْعَمَلِ "

"Whoever testifies that none has the right to be worshipped but Allah, Alone Who has no partners, and that Muhammad is His Slave and Messenger [39]*, and that Jesus is Allah's Slave and Messenger and His Word which He bestowed on Mary and a Spirit created by Him, and that Paradise is true and Hell is true, Allah will admit him into Paradise with the deeds he had done even if those deeds were few"* (Bukhari (3180) and Muslim [41]).

2. The Prophet of Allah (ﷺ) emphasized the significance of following the lead of the Imam of Prayer, especially since 'Imam' literally means 'Leader'; he (ﷺ) said,

> " إِنَّمَا جُعِلَ الْإِمَامُ لِيُؤْتَمَّ بِهِ فَلاَ تَخْتَلِفُوا عَلَيْهِ فَإِذَا رَكَعَ فَارْكَعُوا وَإِذَا قَالَ سَمِعَ اللَّهُ لِمَنْ حَمِدَهُ فَقُولُوا رَبَّنَا لَكَ الْحَمْدُ وَإِذَا سَجَدَ فَاسْجُدُوا وَإِذَا صَلَّى جَالِسًا فَصَلُّوا جُلُوسًا أَجْمَعُونَ وَأَقِيمُوا الصَّفَّ فِي الصَّلاَةِ فَإِنَّ إِقَامَةَ الصَّفِّ مِنْ حُسْنِ الصَّلاَةِ "

"The Imam is made as such so that he is followed. Therefore, do not differ from him, bow when he bows, and say, 'Rabbana laka-l-`hamd ('Our Lord! All thanks are due to You')' if he says 'Sami`a-llahu liman `hamidah ('Allah hears those who glorify Him')'; if he prostrates, prostrate (after him), *and if he prays sitting* (such as because of illness), *pray sitting all together, and straighten the rows for the prayer, because straightening of the rows is amongst those things which make your prayer a correct and perfect one"* (Bukhari [680]).

---

[39] [*Ash-Shahadatan* (the Two Testimonials): To testify that none has the right to be worshiped, except Allah, and that Muhammad is Allah's Prophet and Messenger.]

3. The Prophet (ﷺ) designated a fixed share of *Zakah* (obligatory charity) in the wealth of Muslims, such as this *Hadeeth*,

" فِيمَا سَقَتِ السَّمَاءُ وَالْعُيُونُ أَوْ كَانَ عَثَرِيًّا الْعُشْرُ وَمَا سُقِيَ بِالنَّضْحِ نِصْفُ الْعُشْرِ "

"On a land irrigated by rain water or by natural water channels or if the land is wet due to a nearby water channel, there is one-tenth compulsory (Zakat [charity]); *on the land irrigated by the well, half of one tenth* (i.e. one-twentieth) *is compulsory* (as Zakat on the yield of the land)" (*Bukhari* [1388]; *Muslim* collected a similar *Hadeeth* [1630]).

4. In one of his *Hadeeths*, Allah's Prophet (ﷺ) mentioned two pillars of the Fast: fasting with *Eman*, meaning, having Faith in Allah (ﷻ); and with *I`htisab*, sincerely awaiting the reward with Allah Alone,

" مَنْ صَامَ رَمَضَانَ إِيمَانًا وَاحْتِسَابًا غُفِرَ لَهُ مَا تَقَدَّمَ مِنْ ذَنْبِهِ "

"Whoever fasts Ramadhan in Eman (Faith) *and with I'htisab* (Sincerity), *then his previous sins will be forgiven"* (*Bukhari* [37] and *Muslim* [1268]).

5. During his last `Hajj, the Prophet of Allah (ﷺ) performed the practices and rituals of the `Hajj so that his companions could learn these aspects from him (ﷺ). Jabir Ibn Abdullah (ﷺ) said, "I saw the Prophet (ﷺ) throwing pebbles while riding his camel on the Day of Na`hr (Day of Sacrifice) and saying,

" لِتَأْخُذُوا مَنَاسِكَكُمْ فَإِنِّي لَا أَدْرِي لَعَلِّي لَا أَحُجُّ بَعْدَ حَجَّتِي هَذِهِ "

"Learn your rituals from me, because I do not know whether I will be performing another `Hajj after this `Hajj of mine" (*Muslim* [2286]).

Muhammad's Role in Islam

The Prophet of Allah (ﷺ) died only a few months after that `Hajj` season.

The Prophet of Allah (ﷺ) also emphasized the necessity of performing these and other Islamic actions exactly as he (ﷺ) performed them. For instance, Imam Bukhari [680] reported that the Prophet (ﷺ) ordered his companions to,

" وَصَلُّوا كَمَا رَأَيْتُمُونِي أُصَلِّي "

"Pray as you have seen me pray."

Muhammad (ﷺ), the Prophet of Allah, also instituted the Islamic penal code, such as ruling that those who commit the crime of alcohol-consumption be lashed forty times (*Muslim* [3219]).

Prophet Muhammad (ﷺ) also encouraged his followers to practice the best mannerism, such as by stating that,

" الْبِرُّ حُسْنُ الْخُلُقِ "

"Good conduct is al-Birr (Righteousness)" (*Muslim* [6432]).

Prophet Muhammad (ﷺ) ordered both males and females to dress, eat and give charity modestly,

" كُلُوا وَتَصَدَّقُوا وَالْبَسُوا فِي غَيْرِ إِسْرَافٍ وَلاَ مَخِيلَةٍ "

"Eat, give charity, and dress without excessiveness or arrogance" (A Hasan Hadeeth; *Sahih an-Nasaii*[40] [2558]).

---

[40] [*Sunan an-Nasaii*: Imam Ahmad Ibn Shu`aib an-Nasaii (215-303AH/838-926) collected the *Sunan* (pl. for *Sunnah*) known by his name; *Sunan an-Nasaii* is one of the six major Collections of *Hadeeth*.
***Sahih Sunan at-Nasaii**,* by Shaikh Nasir ad-Deen al-Albani, contains the *Sahih* (authentic) *Hadeeths* found in *Sunan an-Nasaii*, while al-Albani's *Dha`eef Sunan an-Nasaii* contains the *Dha`eef* (weak) *Hadeeths* found in *Sunan an-Nasaii*.]

Introduction to: Muhammad (ﷺ), The Prophet of Mercy

The Islamic economy is built on free trade, justice and fairness. It outlaws all types of injustices and illegal practices, such as, and especially usury.

1. Prophet Muhammad (ﷺ) encouraged trade, when he said,

" التَّاجِرُ الصَّدُوقُ الأَمِينُ مَعَ النَّبِيِّينَ وَالصِّدِّيقِينَ وَالشُّهَدَاءِ "

"(On the Day of Resurrection,) *the truthful, honest merchant will be with the Prophets, the Siddiqin* (truthful ones) *and the Martyrs*" [A *Sahihun li-Ghairihi* [41] *Hadeeth*; *Sahih at-Targheeb wat-Tarheeb* [42] [1782]).

2. Prophet Muhammad (ﷺ) cursed those who deal in usury transactions (*Bukhari* [5505] and *Muslim* [2994]).

To continue, Islam allows Muslims to keep their entire earnings, except for the minimal payment of *Zakat*. The Prophet (ﷺ) said to Mu'adh Ibn Jabal (ﷺ) when he sent him to Yemen,

" إِنَّكَ سَتَأْتِي قَوْمًا أَهْلَ كِتَابٍ فَإِذَا جِئْتَهُمْ فَادْعُهُمْ إِلَى أَنْ يَشْهَدُوا أَنْ لاَ إِلَهَ إِلاَّ اللَّهُ وَأَنَّ مُحَمَّدًا رَسُولُ اللَّهِ فَإِنْ هُمْ أَطَاعُوا لَكَ بِذَلِكَ فَأَخْبِرْهُمْ أَنَّ اللَّهَ قَدْ فَرَضَ عَلَيْهِمْ خَمْسَ صَلَوَاتٍ فِي كُلِّ يَوْمٍ وَلَيْلَةٍ فَإِنْ هُمْ أَطَاعُوا لَكَ بِذَلِكَ فَأَخْبِرْهُمْ أَنَّ اللَّهَ قَدْ فَرَضَ عَلَيْهِمْ صَدَقَةً تُؤْخَذُ مِنْ أَغْنِيَائِهِمْ فَتُرَدُّ عَلَى فُقَرَائِهِمْ فَإِنْ هُمْ أَطَاعُوا لَكَ بِذَلِكَ فَإِيَّاكَ وَكَرَائِمَ أَمْوَالِهِمْ وَاتَّقِ دَعْوَةَ الْمَظْلُومِ فَإِنَّهُ لَيْسَ بَيْنَهُ وَبَيْنَ اللَّهِ حِجَابٌ "

---

[41] [*Sahihun li-Ghairihi*: An otherwise weak *Hadeeth* narration is elevated to the status of *Sahih* (authentic) narrations on account of the combined strength of various chains of narrators reporting the same *Hadeeth*.]

[42] [*At-Targheeb wa-t-Tarheeb mina-l-Hadeethi ash-Shareef*: A famous book on encouraging righteousness and discouraging disobedience to Allah (ﷻ) authored by Imam Abdul 'Adheem Ibn Abdul Qawi al-Mundhiri (581-656AH/1185-1258). *Sahih at-Targheeb wat-Tarheeb*, by al-Albani, contains the authentic *Hadeeths* found in, *at-Targheebu wa-t-Tarheeb*, while al-Albani's, *Dha'eef at-Targheeb wat-Tarheeb*, contains the weak *Hadeeths* found in, *at-Targheeb wa-t-Tarheeb*.]

"You will go to a people of Scripture; when you reach them, invite them to testify that none has the right to be worshipped except Allah and that Muhammad is His Messenger. If they obey you, then tell them that Allah has enjoined five prayers on them to be performed every day and night. If they obey you, then, tell them that Allah has enjoined Sadaqa (Zakah, or charity) *on them to be taken from the rich among them and given to the poor among them. If they obey you, then be cautious! Do not take their best properties* (as Zakah), *and be afraid of the invocation of an oppressed person as there is no barrier between his invocation and Allah."* (Bukhari [1401] and *Muslim* [27])

Muhammad (ﷺ), the Prophet of Allah, legislated various rulings that ensure social harmony and the success of the Islamic Society, from ordaining respect for parents and family law, including preserving family ties, to encouraging mutual kindness and cooperation, kindness to neighbors, respect of other Muslims' lives and property, prohibiting aggression against non-Muslim residents of the Islamic State, outlawing sinning in public, ordaining good conduct and mercy between Allah's creation and reminding mankind of their origin. Here are a few examples from the Prophet's *Sunnah*.

جَاءَ رَجُلٌ إِلَى رَسُولِ اللَّهِ ﷺ فَقَالَ: يَا رَسُولَ اللَّهِ مَنْ أَحَقُّ النَّاسِ بِحُسْنِ صَحَابَتِي قَالَ: "أُمُّكَ" قَالَ: ثُمَّ مَنْ قَالَ "ثُمَّ أُمُّكَ" قَالَ: ثُمَّ مَنْ قَالَ: "ثُمَّ أُمُّكَ" قَالَ: ثُمَّ مَنْ قَالَ: "ثُمَّ أَبُوكَ"

A man came to the Messenger of Allah (ﷺ) and asked him, "O, Allah's Messenger! Who is more entitled to my best companionship (kindness; friendship)?" He (ﷺ) said, "Your mother." The man asked, "Who is next?" He (ﷺ) said, "Your mother." The man asked, "Who is next?" He (ﷺ) said, "Your mother." The man asked, "Who is next?" He (ﷺ) said, "Your father." (*Bukhari* [5514] and *Muslim* [4621])

Introduction to: Muhammad (ﷺ), The Prophet of Mercy

He (ﷺ) also said,

" كُلُّكُمْ رَاعٍ فَمَسْئُولٌ عَنْ رَعِيَّتِهِ فَالأَمِيرُ الَّذِي عَلَى النَّاسِ رَاعٍ وَهُوَ مَسْئُولٌ عَنْهُمْ وَالرَّجُلُ رَاعٍ عَلَى أَهْلِ بَيْتِهِ وَهُوَ مَسْئُولٌ عَنْهُمْ وَالْمَرْأَةُ رَاعِيَةٌ عَلَى بَيْتِ بَعْلِهَا وَوَلَدِهِ وَهِيَ مَسْئُولَةٌ عَنْهُمْ وَالْعَبْدُ رَاعٍ عَلَى مَالِ سَيِّدِهِ وَهُوَ مَسْئُولٌ عَنْهُ أَلاَ فَكُلُّكُمْ رَاعٍ وَكُلُّكُمْ مَسْئُولٌ عَنْ رَعِيَّتِهِ "

"*Everyone among you is a Ra-`in (guardian; ruler) and will be asked about his or her sphere of responsibility. The Amir (ruler) who rulers over the people is a Ra-`in (guardian) and will be asked about his subjects; the husband is a Ra`-in (guardian) over his family and will be asked about them; the wife is a Ra-`in (guardian) over her husband's household and his children and will be asked about them; and a servant is a guardian of his master's property and will be asked about it. Thus, everyone among you is a Ra-`in (guardian; ruler) and will be asked about his or her Ra`iyyah (things or people under their care and guardianship).*" (*Bukhari* [2368] and *Muslim* [3408])

He (ﷺ) also emphasized the religious significance of keeping ties with kith and kin,

" إِنَّ اللَّهَ خَلَقَ الْخَلْقَ حَتَّى إِذَا فَرَغَ مِنْ خَلْقِهِ قَالَتِ الرَّحِمُ هَذَا مَقَامُ الْعَائِذِ بِكَ مِنَ الْقَطِيعَةِ قَالَ نَعَمْ أَمَا تَرْضَيْنَ أَنْ أَصِلَ مَنْ وَصَلَكِ وَأَقْطَعَ مَنْ قَطَعَكِ قَالَتْ بَلَى يَا رَبِّ قَالَ فَهُوَ لَكِ " قَالَ رَسُولُ اللَّهِ ﷺ : " فَاقْرَءُوا إِنْ شِئْتُمْ ﴿ فَهَلْ عَسَيْتُمْ إِن تَوَلَّيْتُمْ أَن تُفْسِدُوا۟ فِى ٱلْأَرْضِ وَتُقَطِّعُوٓا۟ أَرْحَامَكُمْ ۝ ﴾ "

"*Allah created creation and then, when He had finished creating, the Ra`him (womb) said, 'This is the stance taken by that which seeks refuge with You from Qatee`ah (being severed).' Allah said, 'Yes. Will you be satisfied if I keep relations with those who keep your ties and sever relations with those who sever your ties?' The*

Ra`him said, 'Yes, O, my Lord!' Allah said, 'It is granted to you.'" The Prophet (ﷺ) then said, "**Read, if you wish, {Would you then, if you were given the authority, do mischief in the land and sever your ties of kinship?}** [47:22]" (*Bukhari* [5528] and *Muslim* [4634])

He (ﷺ) said, while describing the mercy and kindness that flourishes between the believers,

" تَرَى الْمُؤْمِنِينَ فِي تَرَاحُمِهِمْ وَتَوَادِّهِمْ وَتَعَاطُفِهِمْ كَمَثَلِ الْجَسَدِ إِذَا اشْتَكَى عُضْوًا تَدَاعَى لَهُ سَائِرُ جَسَدِهِ بِالسَّهَرِ وَالْحُمَّى "

"*You see the believers as regards their being merciful, compassionate and kind with each other resembling one body that, if any part of the body is not well, the whole body shares the sleeplessness* (insomnia) *and fever that accompanies it*" (*Bukhari* [5552] and *Muslim* [4685]).

He (ﷺ) asserted the rights of neighbors, by saying,

" مَا زَالَ يُوصِينِي جِبْرِيلُ بِالْجَارِ حَتَّى ظَنَنْتُ أَنَّهُ سَيُوَرِّثُهُ "

"*Jibril* (Angel Gabriel ﷺ) *kept recommending* (reminding) *me to take care of neighbors, until I thought he was going to set a share in the inheritance for them*" (*Bukhari* [5555] and *Muslim* [4756])

He (ﷺ) ordained respect of other Muslims for those who wish to behave like Muslims; he (ﷺ) was once asked about what part of Islam is best, or who is the best Muslim, and he replied,

" مَنْ سَلِمَ الْمُسْلِمُونَ مِنْ لِسَانِهِ وَيَدِهِ "

"*He from whose tongue* (i.e., verbal abuse) *and hand other Muslims are safe*" (*Bukhari* [10] and *Muslim* [59]).

He (ﷺ) also prohibited aggression against non-Muslim residents of the Islamic State,

" مَنْ خَرَجَ مِنَ الطَّاعَةِ وَفَارَقَ الْجَمَاعَةَ فَمَاتَ مَاتَ مِيتَةً جَاهِلِيَّةً وَمَنْ قَاتَلَ تَحْتَ رَايَةٍ عِمِّيَّةٍ يَغْضَبُ لِعَصَبَةٍ أَوْ يَدْعُو إِلَى عَصَبَةٍ أَوْ يَنْصُرُ عَصَبَةً فَقُتِلَ فَقِتْلَةٌ جَاهِلِيَّةٌ وَمَنْ خَرَجَ عَلَى أُمَّتِي يَضْرِبُ بَرَّهَا وَفَاجِرَهَا وَلَا يَتَحَاشَى مِنْ مُؤْمِنِهَا وَلَا يَفِي لِذِي عَهْدٍ عَهْدَهُ فَلَيْسَ مِنِّي وَلَسْتُ مِنْهُ "

"*Whoever defects from obedience* (to the Muslim Leader) *and separates from the community of believers, when he dies, he dies in a state of Jahiliyyah*[43]. *Whoever fights under the banner of people whose cause is not clear* (if just or unjust), *who gets full of family pride, calls* (people) *to fight in the cause of their family honor or fights to support his kith and kin*[44], *and is killed* (for this cause), *then he dies in a state of Jahiliyyah. Whoever indiscriminately attacks my Ummah* (Muslims) *killing the righteous and the wicked among them, sparing not* (even) *those firm in faith and fulfilling not a pledge made with whoever was given a promise of security*[45], *has nothing to do with me and I have nothing to do with him.*"
(*Muslim* [3436])

He (ﷺ) outlawed *Mujaharah* (sinning in public), by saying,

" كُلُّ أُمَّتِي مُعَافًى إِلَّا الْمُجَاهِرِينَ وَإِنَّ مِنَ الْمُجَاهَرَةِ أَنْ يَعْمَلَ الرَّجُلُ بِاللَّيْلِ عَمَلًا ثُمَّ يُصْبِحَ وَقَدْ سَتَرَهُ اللَّهُ عَلَيْهِ فَيَقُولَ يَا فُلَانُ عَمِلْتُ الْبَارِحَةَ كَذَا وَكَذَا وَقَدْ بَاتَ يَسْتُرُهُ رَبُّهُ وَيُصْبِحُ يَكْشِفُ سِتْرَ اللَّهِ عَنْهُ "

"*All the sins of my followers will be forgiven except those of the Mujahirin* (who commit sins openly or disclose their sins to others). *An example of such disclosure* (Mujaharah) *is that a person commits*

---

[43] [*Jahiliyyah*: The Pre-Islamic Era of Paganism and Ignorance.]

[44] [not for Allah's Cause, but for pride in the sake of family, tribe or nationalism]

[45] [meaning, non-Muslims living under the protection of the Islamic State or those who were granted safe passage]

a sin at night and though Allah screens it from the public, then he comes in the morning, and says, 'O so-and-so, I did such-and-such (evil) deed yesterday,' though he spent his night screened by his Lord (none knowing about his sin) and in the morning he removes Allah's screen from himself." (Bukhari [5608] and Muslim [5306])

He (ﷺ) also said,

" لاَ تَبَاغَضُوا وَلاَ تَحَاسَدُوا وَلاَ تَدَابَرُوا وَكُونُوا عِبَادَ اللَّهِ إِخْوَانًا وَلاَ يَحِلُّ لِمُسْلِمٍ أَنْ يَهْجُرَ أَخَاهُ فَوْقَ ثَلاَثَةِ أَيَّامٍ "

"Do not hate one another; do not be jealous of one another; do not desert each other; and, O, Allah's Worshipers! Be brothers. It is not permissible for any Muslim to desert (not talk to) his brother (Muslim) for more than three days." (Bukhari [5605] and Muslim [4641])

He (ﷺ) also reminded mankind of their unity in origin also emphasized in the Quran such as Ayah 49:13 which is mentioned in this Hadeeth,

" وَالنَّاسُ بَنُو آدَمَ وَخَلَقَ اللَّهُ آدَمَ مِنَ التُّرَابِ قَالَ اللَّهُ: ﴿ يَٰٓأَيُّهَا ٱلنَّاسُ إِنَّا خَلَقْنَٰكُم مِّن ذَكَرٍ وَأُنثَىٰ وَجَعَلْنَٰكُمْ شُعُوبًا وَقَبَآئِلَ لِتَعَارَفُوٓا۟ إِنَّ أَكْرَمَكُمْ عِندَ ٱللَّهِ أَتْقَىٰكُمْ إِنَّ ٱللَّهَ عَلِيمٌ خَبِيرٌ ﴾ "

"People are the Children of Adam, and Allah created Adam from dust. Allah said, {O, Mankind! We have created you from a male and a female, and made you into nations and tribes, that you may know one another. Verily, the most honourable of you with Allâh is that (believer) who has at-Taqwâ (the Pious). Verily, Allâh is All-Knowing, All-Aware.}" (A Sahih Hadeeth; Sahih at-Tirmidhi [3270])

Further, he (ﷺ) emphasized the necessity of being merciful to each other and to Allah's creation, including animals,

" الرَّاحِمُونَ يَرْحَمُهُمُ الرَّحْمَنُ ارْحَمُوا مَنْ فِي الأرْضِ يَرْحَمْكُمْ مَنْ فِي السَّمَاءِ "

"The merciful will be granted mercy by the Most Merciful. Be merciful with those on earth and He Who is in heaven will be merciful to you." (A *Sahih Hadeeth*; *Sahih at-Tirmidhi* [1924])

He (ﷺ) encouraged humane treatment of animals in such a profound way as to open the sincere heart and the comprehending mind to the benefits of being righteous even with animals,

" بَيْنَا رَجُلٌ يَمْشِي فَاشْتَدَّ عَلَيْهِ الْعَطَشُ فَنَزَلَ بِئْرًا فَشَرِبَ مِنْهَا ثُمَّ خَرَجَ فَإِذَا هُوَ بِكَلْبٍ يَلْهَثُ يَأْكُلُ الثَّرَى مِنَ الْعَطَشِ فَقَالَ لَقَدْ بَلَغَ هَذَا مِثْلُ الَّذِي بَلَغَ بِي فَمَلأَ خُفَّهُ ثُمَّ أَمْسَكَهُ بِفِيهِ ثُمَّ رَقِيَ فَسَقَى الْكَلْبَ فَشَكَرَ اللَّهُ لَهُ فَغَفَرَ لَهُ " قَالُوا: يَا رَسُولَ اللَّهِ وَإِنَّ لَنَا فِي الْبَهَائِمِ أَجْرًا قَالَ: " فِي كُلِّ كَبِدٍ رَطْبَةٍ أَجْرٌ "

"While a man was walking he felt thirsty and went down a well and drank water from it. On coming out, he saw a dog panting and eating mud because of excessive thirst. The man said, 'This (dog) is suffering from the same problem I was suffering from.' He (went down the well) *filled his shoe with water, held it with his teeth, climbed up and gave water to the dog. Allah thanked him for his* (good) *deed and forgave him.'"* The people asked, "O, Allah's Messenger! Is there a reward for us in serving (the) animals?" He (ﷺ) replied, *"Yes, there is a reward for serving anything animate* (alive)." (*Bukhari* [2190] and *Muslim* [4162])

Prophet Muhammad (ﷺ) encouraged seeking knowledge, especially knowledge of the religion, by saying,

" طَلَبُ الْعِلْمِ فَرِيضَةٌ عَلَى كُلِّ مُسْلِمٍ "

"Seeking knowledge is required from every Muslim" [A *Sahih Hadeeth*; *Sahih Ibn Majah*[46] [184]).

Prophet Muhammad (ﷺ) encouraged both the rulers and the ruled to cooperate for the benefit of the Islamic Nation. He (ﷺ) stated that among the seven whom Allah (ﷻ) will shade on the Day of Judgment when there will be no shade but His Shade, is,

$$\text{" الإِمَامُ الْعَادِلُ "}$$

"Al-Imamu-l-`Adil (the Just Ruler)!" (*Bukhari* [620] and *Muslim* [1712])

He (ﷺ) also ordered Muslims to obey Muslim Leaders, but only in that which is in accordance with obedience to Allah (ﷻ),

$$\text{" السَّمْعُ وَالطَّاعَةُ حَقٌّ مَا لَمْ يُؤْمَرْ بِالْمَعْصِيَةِ فَإِذَا أُمِرَ بِمَعْصِيَةٍ فَلاَ سَمْعَ وَلاَ طَاعَةَ "}$$

"Hearing and obeying is a right as long as one is not ordered to commit a sin in which case there is no hearing or obedience" (*Bukhari* [2735]).

This is because,

$$\text{" إِنَّمَا الطَّاعَةُ فِي الْمَعْرُوفِ "}$$

"Obedience is only with regards to that which is Ma`ruf (part of Islamic righteousness)" (*Bukhari* [6612] and *Muslim* [3424]).

---

[46] [*Sunan Ibn Majah*: Imam Muhammad Ibn Yazid Ibn Majah (209-273AH/824-886) collected the *Hadeeth* Collection known by, *Sunan Ibn Majah,* which is one of the six major Collections of *Hadeeth*.
Sahih Sunan Ibn Majah, by Nasir ad-Deen al-Albani, contains the *Sahih* (authentic) *Hadeeths* found in *Sunan Ibn Majah,* while al-Albani's *Dha`eef Sunan Ibn Majah* contains the *Dha`eef* (weak) *Hadeeths* found in *Sunan Ibn Majah.*]

Regarding warfare, Prophet Muhammad (ﷺ) prohibited targeting civilians in war. Abdullah Ibn Umar (؂) said, "A woman was found dead during one of the Prophet's battles. Consequently, the Messenger of Allah (ﷺ) forbade the killing of women and children" (*Bukhari* [2791] and *Muslim* [3279]).

In the *Quran*, Allah (ﷻ) gave this description for His Messenger (ﷺ),

﴿ وَيُحِلُّ لَهُمُ ٱلطَّيِّبَٰتِ وَيُحَرِّمُ عَلَيْهِمُ ٱلْخَبَٰٓئِثَ ﴾

{*He allows them as lawful at-Tayyibât* (all good and lawful things, deeds, beliefs, persons, foods), *and prohibits them as unlawful al-Khabâ'ith* (all evil and unlawful things, deeds, beliefs, persons, foods)} (7:157).

The Prophet of Allah (ﷺ), whose role includes legislating by permission from Allah as *Ayah* 7:157 indicates, allowed the *Tayyibat* for Muslims and outlawed all types of *Khaba-ith*. This includes modifying the meaning of some of the *Ayat* of the *Quran* to either add to their general implication, by permission from Allah (ﷻ), or restrict their apparent meaning, by permission from Allah (ﷻ).

For instance, Allah (ﷻ) said,

﴿ إِنَّمَا حَرَّمَ عَلَيْكُمُ ٱلْمَيْتَةَ وَٱلدَّمَ وَلَحْمَ ٱلْخِنزِيرِ وَمَآ أُهِلَّ لِغَيْرِ ٱللَّهِ بِهِۦ ﴾

{*He* (Allâh) *has forbidden you only al-Maitah* (meat of a dead animal), *blood, the flesh of swine, and any animal which is slaughtered as a sacrifice for others than Allâh*[47]} (16:115).

---

[47] [or has been slaughtered for idols or on which Allâh's Name has not been mentioned while slaughtering]

Muhammad's Role in Islam

Among the *Tayyibat* that the Prophet (ﷺ) allowed for Muslims in his *Sunnah* are fish and locust, as he stated in this *Hadeeth*,

" أُحِلَّتْ لَكُمْ مَيْتَتَانِ وَدَمَانِ فَأَمَّا الْمَيْتَتَانِ فَالْحُـــوتُ وَالْجَرَادُ وَأَمَّا الدَّمَانِ فَالْكَبِدُ وَالطِّحَالُ "

"You have been allowed two types of dead (animals) *and two types of blood. As for the two dead* (animals), *they are fish and locust; as for the two bloods, they are liver and spleen."* (A Sahih Hadeeth; Sahih Ibn Majah [2695])

Therefore, Prophet Muhammad (ﷺ) excluded these types of foods from the general prohibition found in *Ayah* 16:115, thus, making them part of the *Tayyibat*, good foods, that he was sent to allow for his following.

Among the *Khaba-ith*, unlawful foods, that Prophet Muhammad (ﷺ) forbade for Muslims, is prohibiting eating the meat of donkeys,

" فَلاَ تَطْعَمُوا مِنْ لُحُومِ الْحُمُرِ شَيْئًا "

"Do not eat donkey meat!" (Bukhari [2922] and *Muslim* [3585])

Therefore, Prophet Muhammad (ﷺ) expanded the general implication of *Ayah* 16:115 to include prohibiting consuming the meat of domesticated donkeys, even if properly slaughtered. Zebras, i.e., wild donkeys, are not included in this prohibition. Muslims are allowed to consume zebra meat, by the words of Muhammad (ﷺ) (*Bukhari* [5068]).

Fortieth: As promised, Allah (ﷻ) protected the *Quran* from corruption in various ways.

Allah (ﷻ) explained the *Quran* in detail through Quranic *Ayat* (statements) and by the words of His Messenger (ﷺ),

﴿ قَدْ فَصَّلْنَا ٱلْأَيَٰتِ لِقَوْمٖ يَعْلَمُونَ ۝ ﴾

{*We have* (indeed) *explained in detail Our Ayât* (proofs, evidences, lessons, signs, revelations, etc.) *for people who know*} (6:97).

Allah (ﷻ) also said,

﴿ وَنَزَّلْنَا عَلَيْكَ ٱلْكِتَٰبَ تِبْيَٰنٗا لِّكُلِّ شَيْءٖ وَهُدٗى وَرَحْمَةٗ وَبُشْرَىٰ لِلْمُسْلِمِينَ ۝ ﴾

{*And We have sent down to you* (O, Muhammad ﷺ) *the Book* (the *Qur'ân*) *as an exposition of everything, a guidance, a mercy, and glad tidings for those who have submitted themselves* (to Allâh as Muslims)} (16:89).

Allah (ﷻ) sent an *Ummi* (unlettered) Prophet, Muhammad (ﷺ), to an *Ummi* (unlettered) nation, the Arabs, a nation that relied on memory to preserve its language and traditions and to transfer its language and traditions verbally to the next generation,

﴿ هُوَ ٱلَّذِى بَعَثَ فِى ٱلْأُمِّيِّۦنَ رَسُولٗا مِّنْهُمْ يَتْلُواْ عَلَيْهِمْ ءَايَٰتِهِۦ وَيُزَكِّيهِمْ وَيُعَلِّمُهُمُ ٱلْكِتَٰبَ وَٱلْحِكْمَةَ وَإِن كَانُواْ مِن قَبْلُ لَفِى ضَلَٰلٖ مُّبِينٖ ۝ ﴾

{*He* (Allâh) *it is Who sent among the Ummiyyeena* (unlettered ones) *a Messenger* (Muhammad ﷺ) *from among themselves, reciting to them His Ayat, purifying them* (from the filth of disbelief and polytheism), *and teaching them the Book* (this *Qur'ân*; Islâmic laws) *and al-`Hikmah* (Muhammad's *Sunnah*). *And verily, they had been before in manifest error.*} (62:2)

The entire *Quran* was compiled in one book early on in the Islamic Era. Even though he was *Ummi* (unlettered) himself, under the Prophet's direct and active supervision, the companions (ﷺ) transcribed the *Quran* during his lifetime. He (ﷺ) supervised the recording of the *Quran* from memory, the same memory that Allah (ﷻ) promised to keep the *Quran* inscribed in it,

$$\text{إِنَّ عَلَيْنَا جَمْعَهُ وَقُرْآنَهُ}$$

{*It is for Us to collect it* ('in your heart, O, Muhammad') *and to give you* (O, Muhammad) *its Qur'ân* (the ability to recite *Qur'ân*)} (75:17).

Abu Bakr Ibn Abi Qu'hafah (ﷺ)
The First to Collect the *Quran* in One Manuscript

Abu Bakr Ibn Abi Qu`hafah (ﷺ) was born around 573CE/51 BH, i.e., fifty-one years before the Prophet's *Hijrah*[48]. Abu Bakr (ﷺ) died in 634 CE, corresponding to the 12th year AH, meaning, after the Prophet's *Hijrah*. Abu Bakr (ﷺ) was the Prophet's closest friend for more than forty years, his staunchest supporter and companion, and the father of Aishah, the Prophet's beloved wife (ﷺ). Abu Bakr (ﷺ) became the first *Khaleefah* (Caliph), or Leader of the Islamic State, after the Prophet's death in 10AH/632CE.

After the Prophet of Allah (ﷺ), Abu Bakr (ﷺ) always was, still is and will always be the best Muslim among the *Ummah* (Nation) of Muhammad (ﷺ). Abu Bakr (ﷺ) was distinguished from all other companions by his outstanding qualities, praiseworthy virtues and substantial benefit to Islam and Muslims.

---

[48] [*Hijrah*: The Prophet's migration from Makkah to Madinah in the year 623 CE.]

The Prophet of Allah (ﷺ) often acknowledged Abu Bakr's sincere and profound service to him (ﷺ) personally and to Islam. He (ﷺ) once sat on the *Minbar* (pulpit) and said,

" إِنَّ عَبْدًا خَيَّرَهُ اللَّهُ بَيْنَ أَنْ يُؤْتِيَهُ مِنْ زَهْرَةِ الدُّنْيَا مَا شَاءَ وَبَيْنَ مَا عِنْدَهُ فَاخْتَارَ مَا عِنْدَهُ "

"Allah gave one of His Slaves the choice of receiving whatever he wishes of the splendor and luxury of the worldly life or to accept the good (of the Hereafter) **which is with Allah. He chose that good which is with Allah.**[49]**"**

Abu Bakr (ؓ) wept and said, "May our fathers and mothers be sacrificed for you[50]." Abu Sa`eed al-Khudri (ؓ), the narrator of the *Hadeeth*, said, "We were astonished at this. The people started saying, 'Look at this old man! Allah's Messenger (ﷺ) talks about a Slave of Allah to whom He has given the option to choose either the splendor of this worldly life or the good which is with Him, while he (Abu Bakr) says, 'May our fathers and mothers be sacrificed for you.' But, it was Allah's Messenger (ﷺ) who had been given the option, and among us, Abu Bakr was the most knowledgeable in him (ﷺ)." *Abu Bakr immediately understood that the Prophet (ﷺ) meant himself; this is how intimately and deeply he understood his Prophet (ﷺ).*

Allah's Prophet (ﷺ) added,

" إِنَّ مِنْ أَمَنِّ النَّاسِ عَلَيَّ فِي صُحْبَتِهِ وَمَالِهِ أَبَا بَكْرٍ "

"No doubt, I am indebted to Abu Bakr more than to anyone else regarding both his companionship and his wealth." (*Bukhari* [3615] and *Muslim* [4390])

---

[49] [he chose to die and be with Allah rather than live in luxury in this life]

[50] [Arabs used to say this when they wanted to show love and respect for others.]

Muhammad's Role in Islam

The Prophet of Allah (ﷺ) often asserted Abu Bakr's unrivaled dearness to him. Numerous authentic *Hadeeths* emphasized Abu Bakr's virtues, such as the Prophet's statement describing Abu Bakr as being the dearest man to him (*Bukhari* [4010] and *Muslim* [4396]).

Also, during the lifetime of the Prophet (ﷺ), his companions (رضي الله عنهم) considered Abu Bakr, then Umar Ibn al-Khattab, then Uthman Ibn Affan as being the best Muslims after the Prophet of Allah (ﷺ) (*Bukhari* [3382 & 3421]). The Prophet of Allah (ﷺ) used to hear this statement from his companions and would not object to it (A *Sahih Hadeeth*; *Dhilal al-Jannah*[51] [1193]).

On the advice of Umar Ibn al-Khattab (رضي الله عنه) (41BH-22AH/583-642), Abu Bakr ordered Zaid Ibn Thabit (11BH-51AH/612-671) to collect the *Quran* in one manuscript, saying to him, "You are a wise young man and we do not suspect you (of lying or of forgetfulness); you used to write the Divine Revelation for Allah's Messenger (ﷺ). Therefore, look for the *Quran* and collect it (in one manuscript)." (*Bukhari* [4311])

Zaid (رضي الله عنه), one of the Prophet's close companions, was also among the companions who memorized the *Quran*, as Imams Bukhari [3526] and Muslim [4507] reported. Further, Zaid was one of the numerous scribes who recorded *Quran* for the Prophet (ﷺ), as Imam Bukhari [4605] reported. Imam Bukhari [4606] also reported that the Prophet of Allah (ﷺ) once called Zaid to write *Quran* for him, saying,

" ادْعُ لِي زَيْدًا وَلْيَجِئْ بِاللَّوْحِ وَالدَّوَاةِ وَالْكَتِفِ " ثُمَّ قَالَ: " اكْتُبْ: ﴿ لَا يَسْتَوِي الْقَاعِدُونَ مِنَ الْمُؤْمِنِينَ ﴾ "

---

[51] [*Kitab as-Sunnah*: Imam Abu Bakr Ibn Abi Asim (206-278AH/821-891) collected *Kitab as-Sunnah*, a major *Hadeeth* Collection.
Shaikh Nasir ad-Deen al-Albani wrote, *Dhilal al-Jannah fi Takhreej as-Sunnah*, which contains scientific analysis and criticism of *Hadeeth* narrations found in, *Kitab as-Sunnah*.]

"Call Zaid for me and let him bring the board, the inkpot and the scapula bone[52]." Then he (ﷺ) said [to Zaid], *"Write* [this *Ayah*]: {*Not equal are those of the believers who sit* (at home) ...} [4:95]"

When Abu Bakr entrusted the job of collecting the *Quran* to him, Zaid collected Quranic *Ayat* from people's chests, meaning memory, and from leaves and papers, as Imam Bukhari [4311] reported. As stated, Abu Bakr (ﷺ) died in the twelfth year of the Prophet's *Hijrah*, only two years after the Prophet's death and *after* the job of collecting the *Quran* in one manuscript was completed.

The completed Quranic manuscript collected by Zaid (ﷺ) remained with Abu Bakr (ﷺ) until he died, then with Umar (ﷺ), the second Caliph, until he died, then with Umar's daughter, Hafsah (ﷺ) (17BH-41AH/607-661), the Prophet's wife; this was also reported by Imam Bukhari [4311].

It should be noted that Abu Bakr's manuscript of the *Quran* was meant to be a reference for later generations. Its value is profound because of the fact that it was collected less than two years after the Prophet's death, having been collected by agreement of the Prophet's companions (ﷺ) and in the lifetime of the majority of them. Further, the job of collecting the *Quran* was entrusted to Zaid, who learned the *Quran* directly from the Prophet of Allah (ﷺ) and transcribed the *Quran* by his order; he had also memorized the *Quran* during the Prophet's lifetime.

The manuscript Zaid collected by order from Abu Bakr by no means was the only copy of the *Quran* available to Muslims. Countless number of Muslims, tens of thousands of whom were the Prophet's companions, kept parts or all of the *Quran* in their memory and wrote various parts of it on whatever was available to write on, such as paper, leaves, bones, stones, etc.

---

[52] [instrument used for writing during this age]

Umar Ibn al-Khattab (♦)
The First to Suggest Collecting the *Quran* in One Manuscript

Umar Ibn al-Khattab (♦) ruled the Muslim Nation for ten years after Abu Bakr (♦) died. There are numerous *Hadeeths* that assert the virtues and qualities of Umar, such as his being the second dearest man to the Prophet of Allah (ﷺ), after Abu Bakr (*Bukhari* [4010] and *Muslim* [4396]). The Prophet's companions (♦) used to consider Umar the second best follower of Muhammad (ﷺ) (*Bukhari* [3382 & 3421]).

Umar Ibn al-Khattab (♦) was assassinated by a *Majusi* (fire-worshipper) fanatic, who also killed several other Muslims before taking his own life. Umar (♦) was the Prophet's friend, companion, minister, father-in-law and second successor. Umar (♦) initiated the idea to collect the *Quran* in one manuscript and convinced Abu Bakr (♦) of the value of this work (*Bukhari* [4311]).

Uthman Ibn `Affan (♦)
Collector of the *Quran* in One Universal Manuscript

After the death of Umar (♦), Uthman Ibn Affan (♦) (48BH-35AH/576-655) became the third *Khaleefah* (Caliph). Uthman (♦) was one of the earliest Muslims and married two of the Prophets daughters, the second after the death of the first; he was among those who memorized the *Quran*. The Prophet's companions used to consider Uthman the third best follower of Prophet Muhammad (ﷺ) after Abu Bakr and Umar (*Bukhari* [3382 & 3421]).

The era under discussion was blessed by the presence of tens of thousands of the Prophet's companions (♦), many of them residing in almost every part of the Islamic World. They witnessed the revelation and its practical explanation by the Prophet of Allah (ﷺ). They taught Muslims what the Prophet (ﷺ) taught them, to recite the *Quran* often and to recite parts of it ***aloud*** every day in every Masjid in the Islamic World during three of the five daily obligatory prayers; Muslims recite the *Quran* silently in the other two obligatory prayers.

This is the era when Uthman relied on the very copy of the *Quran* that Abu Bakr had collected and ordered the same man who collected it, Zaid Ibn Thabit, to *again* collect a manuscript of the *Quran* to be used as *the* reference for all future copies of the *Quran*. Once again, Zaid supervised the collection of the *Quran* into one manuscript; from that copy, the *Quran* was recopied many times and each copy sent to a major city or province in the Islamic World.

Thus, the *Quran* was kept and preserved in two distinct and unique ways. The *Quran* was inscribed in the memory of the tens of thousands of the Prophet's companions (ﷺ) who learned the *Quran* directly from him (ﷺ). It also was inscribed on paper, leaves, stones, bones, and so forth, during and after the Prophet's life, until it was collected in one manuscript, which was then used as the universal copy of reference.

Collectors of the *Quran* were the major companions of the Prophet (ﷺ) who accompanied him throughout his Prophethood and learned the *Quran* and *Sunnah* directly from him. Ever since Allah (ﷺ) revealed it, the *Quran* was and still is being recited on a daily basis throughout the year at homes, workplaces, marketplaces, roadways, Islamic festivals, especially during the nights of *Ramadhan*, the month of Fasting, during religious classes, at schools, and in daily prayers at homes and *Masjids*, which are incorrectly called 'Mosques'.

It has always been a great honor for Muslims to become a '`Hafidh', i.e., one who memorized the entire *Quran* by heart. The Prophet of Allah (ﷺ) favorably described those who frequently recite the *Quran*, by saying,

" أَهْلُ الْقُرْآنِ أَهْلُ اللَّهِ وَخَاصَّتُهُ "

"People of the Quran, are Allah's People and His Private Audience"
[A *Sahih Hadeeth; Sahih Ibn Majah* [179]).

The Prophet of Allah (ﷺ) also described the best Muslims in this *Hadeeth*,

" خَيْرُكُمْ مَنْ تَعَلَّمَ الْقُرْآنَ وَعَلَّمَهُ "

"The Best ones among you are those who learn Quran and teach it" (*Bukhari* [4639]).

Once, the Prophet of Allah (ﷺ) appointed a young boy, Amr Ibn Salamah, to lead his people in Prayer, because Amr had memorized more of the *Quran* than anyone else in his tribe; he was six or seven years old at that time (*Bukhari* [3963]).

Imams Bukhari [4697] and Muslim [2554] also reported that once, the Messenger of Allah (ﷺ) asked a man if he had anything to use as bridal gift, *Mahr*, for a woman he wanted to marry. The man did not have anything for *Mahr*. The Prophet (ﷺ) asked him if he had memorized any part of the *Quran*, and the man listed the Quranic chapters he had memorized. The Prophet (ﷺ) used the parts of the *Quran* the man had memorized as his bridal gift (*Mahr*) to his future wife. In his narration, Imam Muslim added that the Prophet (ﷺ) ordered the man to teach the *Quran*, meaning, the parts he had memorized of the *Quran*, to his future wife, as her *Mahr*.

Ever since the dawn of Islam, the dedication of the Muslim *Ummah* (Nation) has been directed to preserving the *Quran* by keeping it alive written on paper and inscribed in the hearts of the believers, male and female. Traditionally, boys and girls start learning *Quran* by heart at an early age. Many Muslim children learn the entire *Quran* by heart before they reach the age of ten. Even if the most learned Muslim Imam errs while reciting *Quran* during prayer, a child of ten-years, either male or female, who is praying behind the Imam may be the one from among the entire congregation to correct the Imam's mistake.

Currently, hundreds of thousands of Muslims memorize the *Quran* by heart. The same manuscript of the *Quran* Uthman entrusted to Zaid to collect, became *the* reference to every single copy of the *Quran* that existed ever since and still exists today. *A Book that has been preserved in this manner from the time it was revealed, both verbally and in writing, cannot be changed by the work of man.*

Old Arabic Script as Compared to Current Uthmani Script

Here is an example of the old Arabic script of *Surat an-Nas*, the last chapter in the *Quran*, used in earlier manuscripts of the *Quran*, followed by the same *Surah* as written in the current Uthmani Script.

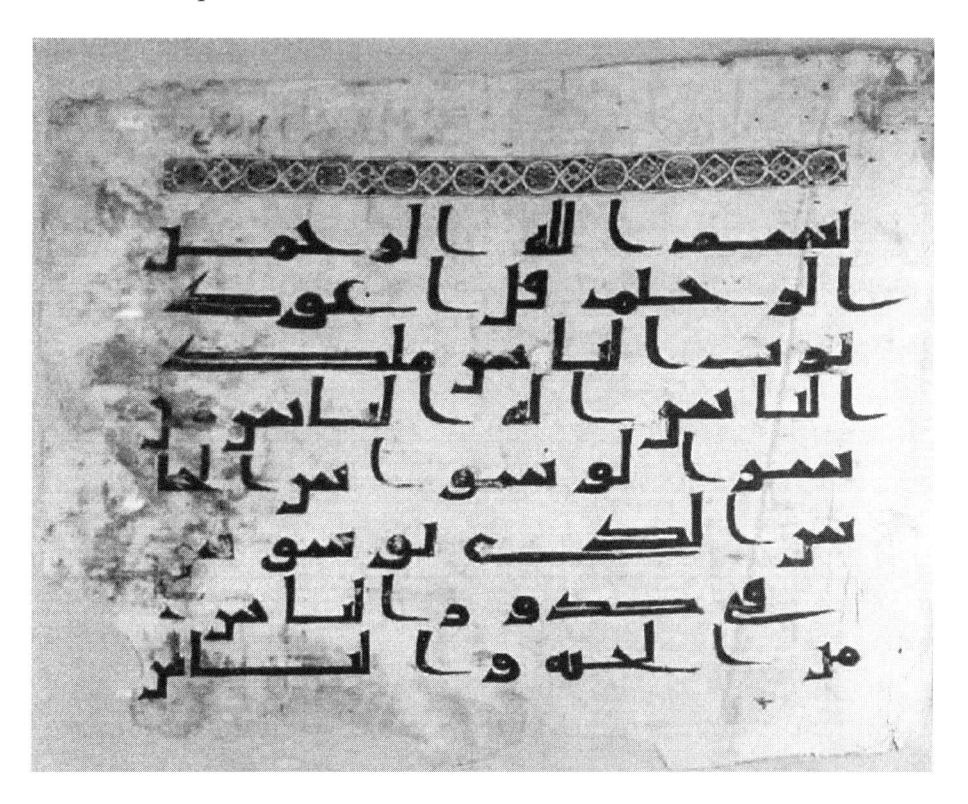

بِسْمِ ٱللَّهِ ٱلرَّحْمَٰنِ ٱلرَّحِيمِ ﴿ قُلْ أَعُوذُ بِرَبِّ ٱلنَّاسِ ۝ مَلِكِ ٱلنَّاسِ ۝ إِلَٰهِ ٱلنَّاسِ ۝ مِن شَرِّ ٱلْوَسْوَاسِ ٱلْخَنَّاسِ ۝ ٱلَّذِى يُوَسْوِسُ فِى صُدُورِ ٱلنَّاسِ ۝ مِنَ ٱلْجِنَّةِ وَٱلنَّاسِ ۝ ﴾

In the Name of Allâh, the Most-Gracious, the Most-Merciful {*Say: "I seek refuge with* (Allâh) *the Lord of mankind. The King of mankind. The Ilâh* ('God') *of mankind. From the evil of the whisperer* (devil, who whispers evil in the hearts of men) *who withdraws* (from his whispering in one's heart after one remembers Allâh). *Who whispers in the breasts* (or hearts) *of mankind. Of Jinn and men.*} (114:1-6)

Ever since Uthman Ibn `Affan, and by agreement from the Prophet's companions, ordered Zaid Ibn Thabit to –again- collect the *Quran* in one manuscript, the Uthmani Manuscript became the basis of every *Quran* copy Muslims have ever had.

This is the eternal miracle of Islam: The Quran, Islam's Holy Book, in addition to the Quran's explanation and meaning, have been preserved for mankind exactly as the Prophet of Islam (ﷺ) *taught them to his companions* (ﷺ).

Forty-First: Allah (ﷻ) **protected the Islamic Message,** *Quran* **and** *Sunnah,* **from corruption; His Prophet** (ﷺ) **completely and entirely delivered Allah's Message and explained it perfectly.**

Prophet Muhammad (ﷺ) explained the religion perfectly; he (ﷺ) said,

" وَايْمُ اللَّهِ لَقَدْ تَرَكْتُكُمْ عَلَى مِثْلِ الْبَيْضَاءِ لَيْلُهَا وَنَهَارُهَا سَوَاءٌ "

"By Allah! I have left you on the white (clear path)*: its night is as bright as its day."* (A Hasan Hadeeth; Silsilat al-A`hadeeth as-Sa`hi`hah [688])

He (ﷺ) also said,

" تَرَكْتُ فِيكُمْ أَمْرَيْنِ لَنْ تَضِلُّوا مَا إِنْ تَمَسَّكْتُمْ بِهِمَا: كِتَابَ اللَّهِ وَسُنَّتِي "

"I have left two matters among you that as long as you hold fast to them you will never go astray: the Book of Allah and my Sunnah" (A *Hasan Hadeeth*; *Manzilatu as-Sunnah*[53] [13]).

The Prophet's companions attested to the fact that He (ﷺ) delivered the Message to them. During his last *Hajj*, in the presence of tens of thousands of his companions, the Prophet of Allah (ﷺ) asked his companions,

" أَلاَ هَلْ بَلَّغْتُ " قَالُوا: نَعَمْ قَالَ: " اللَّهُمَّ اشْهَدْ "

"Did I convey?" They said, *"Yes."* He said, *"O, Allah, be a Witness!"* (*Bukhari* [1625] and *Muslim* [3180])

Forty-Second: Numerous books on the *Quran*'s *Tafsir* (meaning) and *Hadeeth* Collections explain the meaning contained in the *Quran*; *Tafsir* and *Hadeeth* books preserve the *Quran*'s letter and also its *Bayan* (meaning) from corruption.

Muslim Scholars started collecting the *Tafsir* of the *Quran* in the early era of Islam. These include the *Tafsir* of Imam Mujahid Ibn Jabr (20-103AH/640-721CE), who said that he reviewed *Tafsir* of the *Quran* many times with the Prophet's paternal cousin, companion and pupil, Abdullah Ibn Abbas (3BH-68AH/620-687CE). Mujahid said that he asked Ibn Abbas about the meaning of every *Ayah*.

---

[53] [Al-Albani wrote, *Manzilatu as-Sunnati fi-l-Islam wa-Bayanu Annahu la-Yustaghna `Anha bi-l-Quran*: Translated, the title means, 'Status of *Sunnah* in Islam and Proving that the *Quran* Alone Does not Suffice (for Muslims).
This book asserts the necessity of referring to both the *Quran* and the *Sunnah*, not only the *Quran*, for judgment regarding ideas, creeds, acts of worship, code of conduct, and dealings.]

The Prophet of Allah (ﷺ) invoked Allah (ﷻ) to grant knowledge in the religion to his cousin Abdullah Ibn Abbas (*Bukhari* [140] and *Muslim* [4526]). He (ﷺ) also invoked Allah to grant Abdullah Ibn Abbas knowledge in the Book, the *Quran* (*Bukhari* [73]). Allah (ﷻ) accepted His Prophet's invocation. Abdullah Ibn Abbas (ؓ) was among the most knowledgeable companions, especially in the meaning of the *Quran*.

Also included are the *Tafsirs* of Imams Sufyan Ibn `Uyainah (107-198AH/725-813), Abdul Razzaq Ibn Hammam (126-211AH /743-826), Waki` Ibn al-Jarra`h (129-197AH/746-812), Sunaid Ibn Dawud (d. 226AH/840), Is`haq Ibn Rahawaih (161-238AH/777-852), Ahmad Ibn `Hanbal (164-241AH/780-855), Abu Sa`eed al-Ashajj (167-257AH/783-870), `Abd[ul `Hameed] Ibn `Humaid (170-249AH/786-863), Baqei Ibn Makhlad (200-276AH/815-889), Muhammad Ibn Yazid Ibn Majah (209-273AH/824-886), Abu Bakr Ibn al-Mundhir (240-318AH/854-930), Abdul-Ra`hman Ibn Abi `Hatim (240-327AH/854-938), Muhammad Ibn Du`haim (d. 352AH/963), Abu Bakr Ibn Mardawiah (323-410AH/934-1019), and the *Tafsir* books of **Muhammad Ibn Jarir At-Tabari** (224-310AH/839-923) and **Isam`eel Ibn Kathir** (700-774AH/1301-1372).

Countless earlier Muslim Scholars, regardless of whether they wrote on *Hadeeth*, *Fiqh* (Islamic Jurisprudence), or *Seerah* (history), included *Tafsir* of parts or individual *Ayat* from the *Quran* in their books. Rarely, if at all, does one find an Islamic book written by an earlier Muslim Scholar that does not contain a reference to an *Ayah* in the *Quran* where its context is discussed and explained.

The books of *Tafsir* by Imams at-Tabari and Ibn Kathir have become the most popular books of *Tafsir* among those seeking Islamic Knowledge. The *Tafsir* by at-Tabari and Ibn Kathir both explain the *Quran* through the *Quran* itself as well as through the *Sunnah*. Then it is explained by the statements of the Prophet's companions (ؓ), then by the statements of various scholars of Islam, then by the general usage of the Arabic language by those who spoke it proficiently, especially those who first received the *Quran*, the Prophet's generation.

Although the *Quran* itself is infallible and divine, *Tafsir* books are not divine, divinely inspired or immune from error; they are the human effort of those who wrote them, including Imams at-Tabari and Ibn Kathir. It should be noted, though, that these two *Tafsir* books contain a good part of the authentic Islamic traditions in comparison to other books of *Tafsir* in addition to being eloquent and duly researched.

Both at-Tabari and Ibn Kathir were major scholars and Imams of *Sunnah*, *Hadeeth*, *Fiqh* (Islamic Jurisprudence), Arabic language and Islamic history. Their knowledgeable efforts, unique abilities, and eloquent writing style have made their *Tafsir* both popular and respected. As for the error contained in these and other books of *Tafsir*, Muslim Scholars easily identified the erroneous reports and unsubstantiated *Hadeeths* found in them by conducting scientific analysis of their texts and of the chains of narrators reporting them, and declaring weak and fabricated narrations as such.

Forty-Third: The *Quran* was revealed in seven 'A`hruf (Pl. for 'Harf', i.e., way, dialect)', ***all taught by the Prophet himself who was sent with both the Quran and its Bayan*** (meaning).

The Prophet of Allah (ﷺ) said,

" أَقْرَأَنِي جِبْرِيلُ عَلَى حَرْفٍ فَرَاجَعْتُهُ فَلَمْ أَزَلْ أَسْتَزِيدُهُ وَيَزِيدُنِي حَتَّى انْتَهَى إِلَى سَبْعَةِ أَحْرُفٍ "

"*Jibreel* (Angel Gabriel ﷺ) *read the Qur'an to me in one `Hraf* (way; dialect), *so I continued asking him to read it in more `Harfs and he kept doing that, until he read it in seven different A'hruf* (ways; dialects)" (*Bukhari* [4607] and *Muslim* [1355]).

Examples to A`hruf

Imams Bukhari [2241] and Muslim [1354] reported that Umar Ibn al-Khattab (ﷺ) said, "I heard Hisham Ibn Hakim Ibn Hizam recite *Surat-al-Furqan* (chapter 25) in a way different to that of mine. Allah's Messenger (ﷺ) had taught it to me (in a different way). I was about to quarrel with him (during the prayer), but I waited until he finished. Then I tied his garment round his neck, seized him with it, took him to Allah's Messenger (ﷺ), and said, 'I heard him recite *Surat-al-Furqan* in a way different to the way you taught it to me.' The Prophet (ﷺ) ordered me to release him and asked Hisham to recite it. When he recited it, Allah's Messenger (ﷺ) said, '*It was revealed in this way.*' He (ﷺ) then asked me to recite it. When I recited it, he (ﷺ) said,

" هَكَذَا أُنْزِلَتْ إِنَّ الْقُرْآنَ أُنْزِلَ عَلَى سَبْعَةِ أَحْرُفٍ فَاقْرَءُوا مِنْهُ مَا تَيَسَّرَ "

'*It was revealed in this way. The Quran has been revealed in seven different ways, so recite it in the way that is easier for you.*'"

Forty-Fourth: The Prophet's companions (ﷺ) agreed on collecting the *Quran* in one unified manuscript.

As stated, during the *Khilafah* (Caliphate) of Abu Bakr (ﷺ), Zaid Ibn Thabit (ﷺ) was entrusted with the honorable job of collecting the *Quran* in the form of a manuscript. Zaid (ﷺ) collected the *Quran*, each chapter separately, and the resulting manuscript was kept with Abu Bakr (ﷺ) until he died, then with Umar (ﷺ), his successor, until he died, then with Hafsah (ﷺ), Umar's daughter and the Prophet's wife.

During the reign of Uthman (ﷺ), Zaid Ibn Thabit (ﷺ) was again entrusted with collecting a new manuscript of the *Quran* that would be the unified copy Muslims would use all over the World. The same manuscript that Zaid (ﷺ) collected during the *Khilafah* (reign) of Abu Bakr (ﷺ) became *the* reference when the *Quran* was collected again in one manuscript during the *Khilafah* of Uthman (ﷺ), then recopied and sent to major Islamic provinces.

Every copy of the Quran Muslims now have is an exact replica of the Uthmani Manuscript that Zaid collected during the Khilafah of Uthman and which was based on the manuscript Zaid collected during the Khilafah of Abu Bakr.

Points of interest on this topic:

1. Uthman (ﷺ), the Prophet's son-in-law, major companion and third successor, decided to collect the *Quran* in one unified manuscript *after* consulting with the Prophet's companions (ﷺ). `Ali (ﷺ), the Prophet's paternal cousin, son-in-law, major companion and fourth successor, said these words about Uthman, "By Allah, he did not do what he did regarding the *Quran, except by agreement from us.*"[54]

2. Imams Bukhari [5812] and Muslim [4487] collected the Prophet's statement that Angel Jibreel (Gabriel ﷺ) used to review the *Quran* with him once a year, but that year, he said, Jibreel (ﷺ) reviewed the *Quran* with him twice; this indicated the nearness of his death. The Prophet (ﷺ) died that very year.

3. As Imam Ibn Taimiyyah said in his *Fatawa*, this final and most established review is the `Harf that Zaid Ibn Thabit used in the copy of the *Quran* he collected. It is the `Harf Zaid was ordered to collect by Abu Bakr, Umar and Uthman, three of the Four Rightly Guided Caliphs, and agreed to by `Ali, the fourth Rightly Guided Caliph, and the rest of the Prophet's companions (ﷺ). It is the same `Harf Uthman made the unified copy of the *Quran* all Muslims should use, the same copy all Muslims now have and use.

4. The seven methods of reciting Quran, *all of which were taught by*

---

[54] [Imam Ibn Hajar al-Asqalani (773-852AH/1371-1448), a major scholar of *Hadeeth*, stated in his explanation on, *Sahih al-Bukhari*, known as, *Fat`h-ul Bari bi Shar`h-i Sahih-i-l-Bukhari* [8/634], that Ibn Abi Dawud collected `Ali's statement using an authentic chain of narration.]

the Prophet himself, were convenient for the early Muslims and made the *Quran* easy to recite in their own dialects. Soon after the Prophet's death, the Islamic State expanded rapidly and many Arab communities and non-Arabic speaking nations, such as the Turks and the Persians, freely chose to become Muslim and followers of the *Quran* and *Sunnah*. The Prophet's companions (*) realized that if new Muslims and the rest of the Muslim Nation did not unite on one unified manuscript, differences and divisions in the *Quran* itself might appear. This is the reason they agreed with Uthman's decision to have Zaid's manuscript recopied and sent to all Islamic provinces as the one, unified copy of the *Quran* that Muslims have and, ever since, have always had.

5. Uthman completed the magnificent job of collecting the *Quran* in one universal manuscript by ordering that all other copies of the *Quran* be destroyed. Again, it should be noted that `Ali said, "By Allah, he (Uthman) did not do what he did regarding the *Quran, except by agreement from us.*" This is why all Muslims now have access to the Uthmani Manuscript of the *Quran*.

6. Only Allah, the Mighty, the Glorious, can truly appreciate the tremendous service that Abu Bakr, Umar, Uthman, `Ali, Zaid and the rest of the companions did for the benefit of Islam and Muslims when they agreed to Uthman's decision to only use the manuscript that Zaid collected, chosen by their agreement to be the universal copy of the *Quran*.

7. *It should be noted that the other `Harfs of the Quran that the Prophet (*) taught to his companions survived until the present time, available in books of Hadeeth and Tafsir to scholars who use them to offer the variations of meanings for Quranic Texts.* For instance, Imams Bukhari and Muslim collected various parts of `Harfs in the *Tafsir* sections of their collections of *Hadeeth*. Thus, parts of the seven `Harfs are available to all Muslims whenever they read *Hadeeth* Collections of Bukhari and Muslim. However, the copy of the *Quran* that is available to all Muslims wherever they may be is the exact replica of the Uthmani Manuscript.

Introduction to: Muhammad (ﷺ), The Prophet of Mercy

8. The intention behind burning the copies that used the other `Harfs` was not to destroy them completely, but to unify the Muslim Nation on one of the `Harfs` the Prophet (ﷺ) taught to his companions, thus making it available to all Muslims and preventing disputes in the *Quran*. Those who learned other `Harfs` still used their `Harfs`, but, as stated, their `Harfs` were no longer available to the general public.

9. Because he so treasured the '*Harf*' of the *Quran* he directly learned from the Prophet (ﷺ), Abdullah Ibn Mas'ud (ؓ) hesitated at first to agree to taking the 'Quraish `Harf`' that the Prophet's companions (ؓ) agreed upon as the only `Harf` of the *Quran* available to all Muslims.

    a. Imam Bukhari [4616] reported that Abdullah Ibn Mas'ud (ؓ) said, "By Allah, I learned more than seventy *Surahs* (chapters) directly from the mouth of Allah's Prophet (ﷺ)."

    b. In his explanation on Bukhari's *Hadeeth* number 4616, Imam Ibn Hajar al-Asqalani stated that Abdullah Ibn Mas'ud (ؓ) also said that he took the rest of the *Quran* from the Prophet's companions (ؓ). This indicates that Ibn Mas'ud (ؓ) also learned the other companions' `Harfs`; they learned these `Harfs` with the Prophet (ﷺ); there are one-hundred and fourteen *Surahs* in the *Quran*.

    c. Ibn Mas'ud (ؓ) had wished that his `Harf` was used in the unified copy, because of the uniqueness of his `Harf`, saying, "How do you order me to recite the way that Zaid Ibn Thabit learned, when I learned mine from the Prophet's mouth, just as he did?"[55]

    d. In another instance, Ibn Mas'ud complained that he was not entrusted with the job of collecting the *Quran* instead of Zaid Ibn Thabit (A *Sahih* narration; A`hkamu al-Quran[56] [2/608]).

---

[55] [Asqalani, Ibn Hajar. *Fat`h-ul Bari Bi-Shar`h-i Sahih-i-l-Bukhari*.
Imam Ibn Hajar mentioned this statement from Ibn Mas'ud in his explanation on al-Bukhari's *Hadeeth* number 4616.]

[56] [Ibn al-`Arabi, Abu Bakr (d. 543AH/1148). *A`hkamu al-Quran*.]

e. When he realized that his *Harf* was not chosen, Ibn Mas'ud (ﷺ) hesitated in relinquishing his copy of the *Quran*, especially since he learned his `Harf directly from Allah's Prophet (ﷺ).
f. Abdullah Ibn Mas'ud (ﷺ) changed his stance later and agreed with Uthman's decision, which was agreed upon by the community of the Prophet's companions (ﷺ).[57]
g. *It should be made clear that Abdullah Ibn Mas'ud (ﷺ) never said that the Uthmani Manuscript is inaccurate.* Quite the contrary: Imam Ibn Taimiyyah stated in his *Fatawa* that Umar Ibn al-Khattab (ﷺ) ordered Abdullah Ibn Mas'ud (ﷺ) to recite the *Quraish* `Harf in public rather than the *Hudhail* `Harf. Thus, Abdullah Ibn Mas'ud (ﷺ) publicly recited the same `Harf used in the Universal Uthmani Manuscript rather than the `Harf of his own tribe, the Hudhail.
h. Abdullah Ibn Mas'ud (ﷺ) has always had great love and respect in the hearts of the believers. He is worthy of love and respect, being one of the most knowledgeable companions of Muhammad, peace be upon him.
i. The `Harf Abdullah Ibn Mas'ud (ﷺ) learned with the Prophet of Allah (ﷺ) still benefits Muslims until this day. This author often uses parts of Ibn Mas'ud's `Harf that are established by authentic chains of narration to expound on the meaning of various *Ayat* in the *Quran*.
j. What Uthman (ﷺ) did was one of the miracles of Islam, the practical manifestation of Allah's Statement,

﴿ إِنَّا نَحْنُ نَزَّلْنَا ٱلذِّكْرَ وَإِنَّا لَهُۥ لَحَٰفِظُونَ ﴾

{*Verily, We, it is We Who have sent down the Dhikr* (the *Qur'ân*)

---

[57] [Asqalani, Ibn Hajar. *Fat`h-ul Bari bi Shar`h-i Sahih-i-l-Bukhari.*
Imam Ibn Hajar mentioned this report in his explanation on al-Bukhari's *Hadeeth* number 4616.]

and surely, We will guard it (from corruption)} (15:9).

10. It should be noted that the `Harf` that Ibn Mas'ud learned was easier for his tribe, Hudhail, since it was in their own dialect. However, Uthman and the rest of the companions (﷢), including Abdullah Ibn Mas'ud himself later on, agreed to use the *Quraish `Harf*, which Zaid collected.

11. **Quraish:** The pre-eminent Arab tribe; Custodians of the Ka'bah; Rulers of the Islamic Nation for 646 years after the death of the Prophet (ﷺ) in 10AH; The Prophet's own tribe; The Prophet (ﷺ) spoke the Quraish dialect; The last *Quran* review the Prophet (ﷺ) had with Angel Jibreel (ﷇ) was in the Quraish dialect[58], the same `Harf` all Muslims now have and have had ever since Zaid collected it in the unified copy Uthman ordered him to collect.

12. Muslims agree that the Seven *Harfs* in which the *Quran* was revealed, *all of them directly taught by the Prophet* (ﷺ) *who received the Quran from Allah* (ﷻ) *through Angel Jibreel* (Gabriel ﷇ), are all part of Allah's Divine Revelation and contain no contradictions between each other. To the contrary, and as Imam Ibn Taimiyyah stated in his *Fatawa*, the seven `Harfs` are unique to each other in the following four ways.

A'hruf; **various ways of reading the same word:** This type results from different *I`rab*[59] which is generally distinguished by the *Tashkeel*, marks placed above or below Arabic letters to indicate how the letter should be pronounced. Sometimes, by pronouncing and, consequently, writing the same word with different *I`rab* and *Tashkeel* marks, the meaning expands to include various meanings intended in the *Ayah*. Here is an example from *Ayah* 37:12, where

---

[58] [Ibn Taimiyyah, Ahmad Ibn Abdul `Haleem. *Majmu` al-Fatawa*.
Imam Ibn Taimiyyah (661-728AH/1262-1327) was one of the major Muslim Scholars and a polymath of Islamic knowledge.]

[59] [*I`rab* pertains to grammatical rulings of Arabic words and determines how words are pronounced, including what sounds they should be assigned at the end of the word.]

Allah (ﷺ) said,

$$\{ بَلْ عَجِبْتَ وَيَسْخَرُونَ ۝ \}$$

{Bal `Ajibta wa Yas-kharun [Nay, you, (O, Muhammad ﷺ) wondered (at their insolence) while they mock (at you and at the Qur'ân)]} (37:12).

If one reads the word that means 'wondered' with a Fat`hah ( ´ ) at the end عَجِبْتَ, it reads, '`Ajibta', and it means, 'You wondered'. If this word is read with a Dhammah (´) at the end عَجِبْتُ, it would read, '`Ajibtu', and it would mean 'I wondered'. The two meanings are true. In the first instance, Allah (ﷺ) says to his Prophet (ﷺ), "You wondered; while they mock." In the second instance, the statement would mean, "I wondered; while they mock."

Using dots and Tashkeel helps modern-day Muslims read the words of the Quran properly. Early Arab Muslims did not need these tools to know how to pronounce Arabic words properly. They pronounced Arabic words correctly and eloquently since these came to them naturally.

A'hruf; different words that mean the same thing: An example to this type is saying, '`Aq-bil; Halumma; Ta`ala,' to mean, 'Come!' This is the very example that Abdullah Ibn Mas'ud himself gave, as Ibn Taimiyyah stated, to describe this type of difference between various `Harfs.

A'hruf; using a combination of different words that carry different meanings where all of the combinations are true and never contradictory to each other: An excellent example of this type is what the Prophet (ﷺ) himself said, when Ubai Ibn Ka`b (ﷺ) recited an Ayah differently than how Abdullah Ibn Mas'ud (ﷺ) recited it, while a third man recited it in yet a third, different way. They went to the Prophet (ﷺ) and Ubai asked him, "Have you not read such and such Ayah in such and such way?" Abdullah Ibn

Mas'ud also asked the Prophet (ﷺ), "Have you not read such and such *Ayah* in such and such way?" After stating that they all did excellently and beautifully, the Prophet (ﷺ) then said,

" يَا أُبَيُّ إِنِّي أُقْرِئْتُ الْقُرْآنَ ... سَبْعَةَ أَحْرُفٍ لَيْسَ مِنْهَا إِلَّا شَافٍ كَافٍ قُلْتَ غَفُورًا رَحِيمًا أَوْ قُلْتَ سَمِيعًا حَكِيمًا أَوْ قُلْتَ عَلِيمًا حَكِيمًا أَوْ عَزِيزًا حَكِيمًا أَيَّ ذَلِكَ قُلْتَ فَإِنَّهُ كَمَا قُلْتَ مَا لَمْ تَخْتِمْ عَذَاباً بِرَحْمَةٍ أَوْ رَحْمَةً بِعَذَابٍ "

"O, Ubai! The Quran was recited to me [by the Angel from Allah] *... in seven A`hruf* (ways), *each one of them is adequate and sufficient. Whether you said, 'Ghafur-an* (Most-Forgiving), *Ra`heem-an* (Most-Merciful)', *or, 'Samee-'an* (All-Hearer), *`Hakeem-an* (All-Wise)', *or, ' `Aleem-an* (All-Knowing), *`Hakeem-an* (All-Wise)', *or, ' `Azeez-an* (All-Mighty), *`Hakeem-an* (All-Wise)' *if you say any of these, then Allah is all of that. But, do not end punishment with mercy or mercy with punishment."* (A Sahih Hadeeth; at-Tamheed[60] [8/282])

The last part of the Prophet's Statement here means, as another narration for this *Hadeeth* collected by Imam A`hmad in *al-Musnad* (20222) explains, that if an *Ayah* is discussing Allah's Punishment, then one does not mention at the end of it Allah's Attributes that talk about His Mercy, such as Him being the Most-Forgiving, Most Merciful. If an *Ayah* is discussing Allah's Mercy, one does not mention at the end of it Allah's Attributes about His being Severe in punishment. One should mention Allah's Names and Attributes in their proper context.

A'hruf; words that are generally the same, or from the same root word, similar in meaning in some aspects but diverse in meaning in other aspects, especially if different *Tashkeel* (grammatical marks) is applied: Allah (ﷻ) said in *Ayah* 2:222,

---

[60] [Ibn Abdul Barr, Abu Umar (b. 368-d. 463AH/978-1070). At-Tamheed.]

﴿ وَيَسْـَٔلُونَكَ عَنِ ٱلْمَحِيضِ ۖ قُلْ هُوَ أَذًى فَٱعْتَزِلُوا۟ ٱلنِّسَآءَ فِى ٱلْمَحِيضِ ۖ وَلَا تَقْرَبُوهُنَّ حَتَّىٰ يَطْهُرْنَ ۖ ﴾

{*They ask you* (O, Muhammad ﷺ) *concerning menstruation. Say: that is an Adha*[61]; *therefore, keep away from women during menses and go not unto them until they Yat-hurna.*} (2:222)

In the context of this *Ayah*, 'يَطْهُرْنَ (*Yat-hurna*)', means, 'are purified from their menses'. This word shares the same root word as 'يَطَّهَّرْنَ (*Yattaharna*)', which in the context of this *Ayah* means, 'purify themselves from their menses, by taking the required *Ghusl* shower'. Thus, both of these words have a shared meaning that pertains to purity; they both are used in the *Ayah*. However, each of the two words has a distinct meaning: the first, *Yat-hurna*, pertains to physical purity attained at the end of the menses period; the second, *Yattaharna*, pertains to purity attained by taking the *Ghusl* shower at the end of the menses, thus, allowing women to resume praying.

It should be noted here that Allah's Mercy with women is profound. Muslim women are not allowed to pray during menses, but are also not required to make up for missed prayers because of the menses. Aishah (ﷺ) said, "We passed through this (period of menstruation), and we were ordered to make up for the fast, but were not ordered to make up for the prayers" (*Muslim* [508]).

13. It should be noted that, as Imam Ibn Taimiyyah stated in his *Fatawa*, the order of the chapters in Ibn Mas'ud's copy and even Zaid's own copy of the *Quran* was different than the Uthmani Manuscript, since the order of the chapters is a matter of

---

[61] [a harmful thing for a husband to have sexual intercourse with his wife while she is having her menses]

individual judgment. However, the order of *Ayat* in each *Surah* is exactly the same no matter the *`Harf*, because it is a matter of revelation.

14. Ibn Taimiyyah also stated that, according to Muslim Scholars, it is not required for Muslims to recite the *Quran* according to only one of the seven *Harfs*. ***All the seven Harfs came from Allah (ﷺ), are a part of the Quran, and were taught by the Prophet (ﷺ) to his companions (ﷺ).*** The companions chose to make one *`Harf* available to all Muslims to avoid differences and divisions between Muslims and to make it easy for new Muslims who did not speak fluent Arabic to recite the *Quran* accurately.

Forty-Fifth: An example of *Tafsir-ul-Quran*.

Allah (ﷺ) said in the *Quran*,

﴿ قُلْ يَٰٓأَهْلَ ٱلْكِتَٰبِ تَعَالَوْا۟ إِلَىٰ كَلِمَةٍ سَوَآءٍۭ بَيْنَنَا وَبَيْنَكُمْ أَلَّا نَعْبُدَ إِلَّا ٱللَّهَ وَلَا نُشْرِكَ بِهِۦ شَيْـًٔا وَلَا يَتَّخِذَ بَعْضُنَا بَعْضًا أَرْبَابًا مِّن دُونِ ٱللَّهِ ۚ فَإِن تَوَلَّوْا۟ فَقُولُوا۟ ٱشْهَدُوا۟ بِأَنَّا مُسْلِمُونَ ۝ ﴾

{*Say* (O, Muhammad ﷺ): *"O, People of the Scripture: Come to a word that is just between us and you, that we worship none but Allâh* (Alone), *and that we associate no partners with Him, and that none of us shall take others as lords besides Allâh." Then, if they turn away, say: "Bear witness that we are Muslims."*} (3:64)

In his *Tafsir*, Imam Ibn Kathir explained this *Ayah*, by saying, "This *Ayah* pertains to the People of the Book, the Jews and Christians, and those who follow their ways. ... {*Say: "O, People of the Scripture! Come to a word..."*}: 'Word', in Arabic, also means a complete sentence (statement), as evident from this *Ayah*; ... {*"...that is the same between us and you..."*}, means, 'an honest and righteous word that is fair to both sides.' Next, Allah (ﷺ)

explained this 'word', by saying, {"*...that we worship none but Allah (Alone), **and that we associate no partners with Him**...*"), i.e., 'we worship neither a statue, cross, an idol, a *Taghut* (false gods; people) or fire, nor do we worship anything else. We only worship Allah, Alone, without partners'. This is the message of all of Allah's Messengers; Allah (ﷻ) said,

﴿ وَلَقَدْ بَعَثْنَا فِى كُلِّ أُمَّةٍ رَّسُولاً أَنِ ٱعْبُدُواْ ٱللَّهَ وَٱجْتَنِبُواْ ٱلطَّـٰغُوتَ ﴾

{*And verily, We have sent among every Ummah* (community; nation) *a Messenger* (proclaiming)*: "Worship Allâh* (Alone)*, and avoid* (shun) *Tâghût* (all false deities)"} (16:36).'"

Ibn Kathir continued, by saying, "Next, Allah (ﷻ) said [that Muslims should say], {"*...and that none of us shall take others as lords besides Allah.*"} [While explaining this part of the *Ayah*, Tafsir Scholar Abdul Malik] Ibn Juraij[62] said, 'We [Muslims] do not obey each other in disobedience to Allah[63].' Allah (ﷻ) said, next, {***Then, if they turn away, say: "Bear witness that we are Muslims"***), i.e., 'If they (People of the Book) ignore this just call, then let them know that you (Muslims) will remain in Islam as Allah (ﷻ) ordained for you.' We should mention that the letter the Prophet (ﷺ) sent to [the Byzantine Emperor] Heraclius reads [like this],

" بِسْمِ اللَّهِ الرَّحْمَنِ الرَّحِيمِ مِنْ مُحَمَّدٍ رَسُولِ اللَّهِ إِلَى هِرَقْلَ عَظِيمِ الرُّومِ سَلاَمٌ عَلَى مَنِ اتَّبَعَ الْهُدَى أَمَّا بَعْدُ فَإِنِّي أَدْعُوكَ بِدِعَايَةِ الإِسْلاَمِ أَسْلِمْ تَسْلَمْ وَأَسْلِمْ يُؤْتِكَ اللَّهُ أَجْرَكَ مَرَّتَيْنِ فَإِنْ تَوَلَّيْتَ فَإِنَّ عَلَيْكَ إِثْمَ الأَرِيسِيِّينَ وَ ﴿ يَـٰٓأَهْلَ ٱلْكِتَـٰبِ تَعَالَوْاْ إِلَىٰ كَلِمَةٍ

---

[62] [(80-150AH/699-767CE)]

[63] [because only Allah and His Messenger legislate for Muslims]

Introduction to: Muhammad (ﷺ), The Prophet of Mercy

$$\text{سَوَاءٍ بَيْنَنَا وَبَيْنَكُمْ أَلَّا نَعْبُدَ إِلَّا اللَّهَ وَلَا نُشْرِكَ بِهِ شَيْئًا وَلَا يَتَّخِذَ بَعْضُنَا بَعْضًا أَرْبَابًا مِّن دُونِ اللَّهِ ۚ فَإِن تَوَلَّوْا فَقُولُوا اشْهَدُوا بِأَنَّا مُسْلِمُونَ}$$

'In the Name of Allah, the Most-Gracious, the Most-Merciful. From Muhammad, the Messenger of Allah, to Heraclius, Leader of the Romans[64]: Peace be upon those who follow the true guidance. Furthermore I invite you to Islam. Embrace Islam, and if you do, you will acquire safety[65]; embrace Islam and Allah will grant you double your reward[66]. However, if you turn away from Islam, then you will carry the burden of the peasants[67], and, {"O, People of the Scripture! Come to a word that is the same between us and you, that we worship none but Allah (Alone); that we associate no

---

[64] [During that era, Europeans in general were called 'Romans' by the Arabs.]

[65] [In his explanation of Bukhari's *Hadeeth* number 6, Imam Ibn Hajar al-Asqalani said that it was reported that Heraclius said, "By Allah! I know that he (Muhammad ﷺ) is a sent Prophet. However, I fear the Roman people for my life. Otherwise, I would have followed him (Muhammad ﷺ)." Ibn Hajar then said, "Heraclius should have paid attention to the Prophet's statement, '*Become a Muslim and you will acquire safety.*' ... Had he become Muslim, Heraclius would have acquired safety from all that he feared.'" (Asqalani, Ibn `Hajar. *Fat`h-ul Bari bi Shar`h-i Sahih-i-l-Bukhari*)]

[66] [The Prophet of Allah (ﷺ) said that among the three who will be granted double their reward is,

" وَمُؤْمِنُ أَهْلِ الْكِتَابِ الَّذِي كَانَ مُؤْمِنًا ثُمَّ آمَنَ بِالنَّبِيِّ صَلَّى اللَّهُ عَلَيْهِ وَسَلَّمَ فَلَهُ أَجْرَانِ "

"*A believer from among the People of the Book, who was a believer* (in his own book and his own prophet) *and then believed in the Prophet* (Muhammad ﷺ), *he* (or she) *will be granted double his reward*" (Bukhari [2789] and *Muslim* [219]).]

[67] [The Prophet of Allah (ﷺ) said,

" فَالْأَمِيرُ الَّذِي عَلَى النَّاسِ رَاعٍ وَهُوَ مَسْئُولٌ عَنْهُمْ "

"*The Amir* (ruler) *who rulers over the people is a Ra-`in* (guardian) *and will be asked about his subjects*" (Bukhari [2368] and *Muslim* [3408]).]

partners with Him; and that none of us shall take others as lords besides Allah." Then, if they turn away, say: "Bear witness that we are Muslims."} (3:64)" (*Tafsir Ibn Kathir*; the *Hadeeth* on the Prophet's message to Heraclius is also found in *Bukhari* [4188] and *Muslim* [3322])

Forty-Sixth: Allah (ﷻ) protected the *Sunnah* from corruption.

The very people who fulfilled Allah's Promise to protect the *Quran* by memorizing it perfectly, recording it on paper, stone, bones and leaves, then collecting it in one universal manuscript, are the very people who preserved the *Bayan* of the *Quran* and the Prophet's *Sunnah* which he (ﷺ) taught them; he (ﷺ) was sent to do just that,

$$\left\{ وَمَا أَنزَلْنَا عَلَيْكَ الْكِتَابَ إِلَّا لِتُبَيِّنَ لَهُمُ الَّذِي اخْتَلَفُوا فِيهِ ۙ وَهُدًى وَرَحْمَةً لِقَوْمٍ يُؤْمِنُونَ \right\}$$

{*And We have not sent down the Book* (the *Qur'ân*) *to you* (O, Muhammad ﷺ), *except that you may explain clearly unto them those things in which they differ, and* (as) *a guidance and a mercy for a people who believe*} (16:64).

Allah (ﷻ) blessed the Prophet's companions (ﷺ) with exceptional capabilities of memorizing and preserved the *Quran* and His Prophet's *Hadeeth* in their memory. Just like their Prophet, the companions belonged to a largely unlettered nation that relied on memory to preserve its traditions and culture. The Prophet's companions were also trustworthy in conduct and reliable with regards to mental strength. In addition to having recorded the *Quran* in writing under the Prophet's supervision, the Prophet's companions (ﷺ) also recorded parts of the *Sunnah* in writing with the Prophet's permission (A *Sahih Hadeeth*; *Sahih Sunan Abi Dawud* [3645]).

The *Tabi`un*, the second generation of Islam, took the *Quran* from the Prophet's companions (ﷺ) both verbatim and in writing, and they also took the *Quran's Bayan* and the Prophetic *Sunnah* from the Prophet's companions both verbatim and partly in writing. The *Tabi`u at-Tabi`in*, the third generation of Islam, received knowledge of the *Quran* and *Sunnah* from the *Tabi`un* and then transferred it to mankind, generation after generation, orally and in writing.

Recording knowledge of the *Quran* and *Sunnah* in memory and in writing went side by side, with special emphasis on memorizing because it was both the tool and the gift that the Arab nation was endowed with for recording its history and traditions. Soon after, the quality of excellent memorization ability was transferred to and shared by the many nations that accepted Islam. Numerous scholars, Arabs and non-Arabs, appeared throughout the Muslim World and continued the honorable work started by the Prophet's companions (ﷺ) and those who followed them with excellence.

To emphasize these points, we should state that the most respected *Hadeeth* Collection in Islam, Bukhari's *Sahih*, was written by a non-Arab who otherwise had a profoundly efficient and eloquent knowledge of Arabic and Islam. Arabic became the language of Islam, and as such, was no longer the property of Arabs. It became the property of all those who attested to Allah's Oneness and to His Prophet's Prophethood. This is the fruit of the Islamic Message and the manifestation of Allah's Statement,

﴿ يَٰٓأَيُّهَا ٱلنَّاسُ إِنَّا خَلَقْنَٰكُم مِّن ذَكَرٍ وَأُنثَىٰ وَجَعَلْنَٰكُمْ شُعُوبًا وَقَبَآئِلَ لِتَعَارَفُوٓا۟ إِنَّ أَكْرَمَكُمْ عِندَ ٱللَّهِ أَتْقَىٰكُمْ ﴾

{*O, Mankind! We have created you from a male* (Adam) *and a female* (`Hawwa [Eve]), *and made you into nations and tribes, that you may know one another. Verily, the most honorable of you with Allâh is that* (believer) *who has at-Taqwâ* (piety)].} (49:13)

As time passed, the letter of the *Quran* and *Sunnah* and the knowledge associated with them were recorded on an ever-larger scale, both in practice and in written and verbal teaching. All this started during the Prophet's lifetime. The height of this effort during the lifetime of the prophet's companions was their agreement to collect the *Quran* in one manuscript, the *Uthmani* Manuscript, which was copied throughout the Muslim World.

Forty-Seventh: Numerous *Hadeeth* Collections recorded and transcribed the Prophet's *Sunnah*, and consequently, preserved the *Sunnah* from corruption.

Just as Allah (ﷻ) protected the *Quran* from corruption orally and through the *Uthmani* Manuscript that has become the one and only universal copy among Muslims, He (ﷻ) also protected the *Quran's Bayan* and the Prophetic *Sunnah* from corruption orally and through books of *Hadeeth*.

Numerous companions excelled in memorizing *Hadeeth* narrations precisely, just as they memorized the *Quran* either partially or totally. The Prophet's companions who memorized *Hadeeth* word for word include Abu Bakr, Umar, Uthman, `Ali Ibn Abi Talib (23BH[68]-40AH[69]/601-660CE), Sa'd Ibn Abi Waqqas (27BH-55AH/597-674), Anas Ibn Malik, Abu Hurairah (21BH-57AH/603-676), `Aishah (the Prophet's wife), Jabir Ibn Abdullah (17BH-77AH/607-696), Abdullah Ibn `Umar (12BH-73AH/611-692), Abdullah Ibn `Amr (35BH-63AH/589-682), Abdullah Ibn Abbas (3BH-67AH/620-686), Abdullah Ibn az-Zubair (1-73AH/622-692), among countless others. The Prophet's *Hadeeth* was collected from thousands of his companions, may Allah be pleased with all of them.

---

[68] [**BH**: Before the Prophet's *Hijrah*, meaning, the Prophet's migration from Makkah to Madinah in the year 623 CE]

[69] [**AH**: After the Prophet's *Hijrah*]

By definition, the Prophet's companions (ﷺ) had an audience with him (ﷺ) at least once. In his *Sahih*, Imam Bukhari said that whoever among Muslims accompanied the Prophet (ﷺ) or saw him is among his companions. If there is a companion, whether male or female, who could be described as having seen the Prophet (ﷺ) for the least time, the least he or she could do is report the physical description of Allah's Final and Last Prophet and Messenger (ﷺ).

For instance, Imam Muslim [4315] reported that the last among the Prophet's companions to die was Abu at-Tufail, Amir Ibn Wathilah, who died in 728CE, one hundred and ten years after the Prophet's *Hijrah*. Amir was asked if he saw the Prophet of Allah (ﷺ), and he said, "Yes. He was white, and he had a handsome face." Thus, Amir is mentioned among the Prophet's companions, even though when the Prophet (ﷺ) died, Amir was only eight years old (*Tarikh al-Bukhari* [6/446]).

Collecting and recording *Hadeeths* began during the lifetime of the Prophet (ﷺ), with his permission. For instance, he (ﷺ) gave permission to some of his companions to record *Hadeeth* in writing, such as the family of Amr Ibn `Hazm (according to a *Sahih Hadeeth*; *Sahih Sunan an-Nasaii* [4861]), and, Abdullah Ibn `Amr Ibn al-`Aas (according to a *Sahih Hadeeth*; *Sahih Sunan Abi Dawud* [3645]).

Numerous *Hadeeth* manuscripts started to appear early in the Islamic era. They include *Hadeeth* collections by these major Imams and scholars: Al-Hasan al-Basri (21-110AH/641-728), Hammam Ibn Munabbih (born before 34-132AH/before 654-749CE), Ayyub as-Sikhtiyani (68-131AH/691-754), Malik Ibn Anas (93-179AH/716-802), Abdullah Ibn al-Mubarak (118-181AH/741-804), Abu Dawud at-Tayalisi (124-204AH/747-827), Abdul Razzaq Ibn Hammam (126-211AH/749-834), Muhammad Ibn al-`Hasan ash-Shaibani (131-189AH/754-812), Ahmad Ibn `Hanbal (164-241AH/787-864), Muhammad Ibn Sa`d (168-230AH/791-853), Muhammad Ibn Isma`eel al-Bukhari (194-256AH/817-879), Abu `Hatim Muhammad Ibn Idris ar-Razi (195-277AH/818-900), Abu Zur`ah `Ubaidullah ar-Razi (200-264AH/823-887), Muhammad Ibn Nasr al-Marwazi (202-294AH/825-917), Abu Dawud as-Sujustani

(202-275AH/825-898), Muslim Ibn al-`Hajjaj al-Qushairi (204-261AH/827-884), Abu Abdullah Muhammad Ibn Yazid Ibn Majah (209-273AH/832-896), Muhammad Ibn `Eesa at-Tirmidhi (210-279AH/833-902), Ahmad Ibn Shu`aib an-Nasaii (215-303AH/838-926), Abdul-Ra`hman Ibn Abi `Hatim (240-327AH/863-950), Sulaiman Ibn Ahmad at-Tabarani (260-360AH/883-983), Abu `Hatim Ibn `Hibban (270-354AH/893-977), to name a few.

Hadeeth Scholars mentioned here include those from the *Tabi'un* generation who collected *Hadeeth* narrations from the Prophet's companions, may Allah be pleased with all of them. This list is by no means a full view or indication of the tremendous efforts by the early generations of Islam to preserve Islam and transfer it to future generations. If we were to list only the notable *Hadeeth* Collectors from the era under discussion, we would collect large volumes of biographies. Each of the scholars mentioned here had numerous teachers and numerous students; the same is true for their teachers and students.

Hadeeth Collections contain the Prophet's statements and actions as narrated by his companions (ﷺ), who then transmitted *Hadeeth* to their students, who transmitted them to their students, and so forth. They are, more often than not, a repetition of the same *Hadeeth* texts found in other *Hadeeth* Collections, either by repeating the same chains of narrators or by reporting different chains of narrators. Many of these books also contain the religious verdicts of the Prophet's companions (ﷺ). *Hadeeth* Collections mainly contain authentic *Hadeeths*, but they also contain weak and rejected *Hadeeths* often to expose their weaknesses and refute their narrators. The decision to accept a *Hadeeth* as authentic, weak, or fabricated is a scientific decision taken up by experts in the field.

The Muslim Nation has agreed that the most authentic books after the *Quran*, the Book of Allah, are *Hadeeth* Collections of Imam Bukhari then Imam Muslim. They are called, *as-Sa`hi`han*, which literally means, *The Two Sahihs*, or, 'The Two Authentic Collections'.

Forty-Eighth: *Isnad* is a superb scientific method with which the Muslim Nation can and did preserve the letter and the meaning of Islam's two resources, the *Quran* and the *Sunnah*.

To preserve the integrity of the *Sunnah* and the *Quran's* practical *Bayan* (explanation), Muslim Scholars devised an outstanding and scientifically precise method of protecting the Prophetic Tradition from corruption. It is called the method of, '*Isnad*', meaning, using chains of narrators to establish the validity, or lack thereof, of any statement or action attributed to the Prophet (ﷺ). Here is an explanatory example.

A Rare *Hadeeth* Narration

Imam Malik Ibn Anas (93-179AH/711-795), who collected, *al-Muwatta*, was the teacher of **Imam Muhammad Ibn Idris ash-Shafi`i** (150-204AH/767-819), who collected a *Musnad* that carries his name; ash-Shafi'i was the teacher of **Imam A`hmad Ibn `Hanbal** (164-241AH/780-855), who collected the famous *Hadeeth* Collection simply known as, *al-Musnad*. All three of these Imams were major scholars of *Hadeeth*, *Fiqh* (Islamic Law) and other Islamic aspects. It should be noted that, *Musnad*, shares the same root word as *Isnad*.

Example to *Isnad*: Here is a rare *Hadeeth* narration that Imam Ahmad Ibn `Hanbal collected in his *Musnad*, *Hadeeth* number 5597; this *Hadeeth* is also found in, *al-Muwatta*, by Imam Malik [1188].

Imam Ahmad Ibn `Hanbal said, "Muhammad Ibn Idris ash-Shafi'i, may Allah grant him His Mercy, narrated to us saying, 'Malik [Ibn Anas] reported to us from Nafi` from Abdullah Ibn Umar, that the Messenger of Allah (ﷺ) said,

" لاَ يَبِعْ بَعْضُكُمْ عَلَى بَيْعِ بَعْضٍ "

'Let not some of you spoil the sales of some others.'

This *Hadeeth* prohibits spoiling the business transactions of others, such as by saying to the buyer, "Cancel the deal you had with so and son, and I will give you the same product for a cheaper price," or by saying, "I will give you a better product than the one you are buying from so and so, but for the same price."[70]

In the example provided here from, *al-Musnad*, Imam Ahmad narrated this *Hadeeth* from Imam Shafi'i, his teacher, who narrated the *Hadeeth* from Imam Malik, his teacher. Imam Malik reported this *Hadeeth* by mentioning the name of his teacher, Nafi' [d. 117AH/735], Abdullah Ibn Umar's famous student, and Nafi` mentioned the name of his teacher, Abdullah Ibn Umar, the Prophet's companion, who narrated the Prophet's statement. Malik was from the third generation of Islam; only two narrators were between him and the Prophet (ﷺ) in many of the *Hadeeths* he collected.

It should be noted that Imam Malik verbally reported the portion of the *Hadeeth* quoted here using two different chains of narrators, including the one from Nafi`, from Abdullah Ibn Umar. In addition, other *Hadeeth* Collections, such as *Bukhari* [2006], *Muslim* [2786; 2790], *an-Nasaii* [4420], *Abu Dawud* (2979; 2986), Ahmad's *Musnad* [4302; 5597; 8581], and so forth, also collected the portion of the *Hadeeth* quoted here through Malik, some of them reporting both of Malik's chains of narrators. Imam Malik himself reported the two different chains of narrators for the portion of the *Hadeeth* under discussion in his own, *al-Muwatta* [1188; 1189]. **There are literally hundreds of chains of narrators connected in a similar manner as Malik, Shafi`i, A`hmad are connected.**

After a *Hadeeth* Collector transmits his narrations using the chains of narrators through which he obtained *Hadeeth* narrations,

---

[70] [Nawawi, Ya`hya Ibn Sharaf. *Shar`h Sahih Muslim*.
Shar`h Sahih Muslim, is an-Nawawi's explanation on *Hadeeth* narrations found in *Sahih Muslim*; this is the explanation of Muslim's *Hadeeth* number 2786.]

Introduction to: Muhammad (ﷺ), The Prophet of Mercy

Hadeeth Scholars analyze every *Hadeeth*'s chain of narrators, verifying the trustworthiness of every narrator by researching the narrator's history, conduct and how contemporary scholars portrayed his or her character, state of mind and reliability. *Hadeeth* Scholars also verify the continuity of every chain of narrators, until it reached the Prophet (ﷺ), to uncover any missing names in the chain that might disrupt its continuity. Only then, when a chain of narrators is held as acceptable and the text it reports is found accurate and both are also verified as being free from hidden or apparent defects, will a *Hadeeth* be accepted as authentic. In Islam, weak and fabricated *Hadeeths* are rejected. In his introduction to his *Sahih*, Imam Muslim emphasized the necessity of reporting only authentic *Hadeeths*.

Hadeeth reports that do not withstand the rigors of the method of *Isnad* are rejected if they do not have verifiable, continuous and sound chains of narrators that are free from any hidden or apparent defects.[71]

For various reasons, many people have invented statements and reports and attributed them to the Prophet (ﷺ). However, *Hadeeth* Scholars have always been able to easily and skillfully expose and refute invented statements and reports, by relying on *Isnad* and by studying every *Hadeeth*'s context as whether to accept or reject various narrations.

Even when literacy became widespread in the Muslim World, scholars of early and successive Muslim generations relied on memory to preserve *Hadeeth* narrations, as well as, compiling and transcribing *Hadeeth* on a massive professional scale. Just like the *Quran*, the *Sunnah* was preserved through two ingenious methods that separately and jointly preserved its integrity, accuracy and continuity: **Scribing** *Hadeeth* narrations by recording *Hadeeth* reports along with the chains of narrators reporting them,

---

[71] [Albani, Muhammad Nasir ad-Deen. *Al-Hadeethu `Hujjatun bi-Nafsihi fi-l-A`hkami wa-l-`Aqa-id* (The *Hadeeth* is Proof Itself in Matters of Law and Creed) (Pg., 6-7).]

and, preserving *Hadeeth* reports through **memorizing** them and transmitting them from memory along with the chains of narrators reporting them.

For instance, Imam Ahmad Ibn `Hanbal memorized around two million narrations of Prophetic *Hadeeths* and statements and religious verdicts of the Prophet's companions and the two successive generations; *the narrations Ahmad memorized included the chains of narrators.* However, these are *not* two million different *Hadeeths* said by the Prophet (ﷺ). They include various narrations reporting the same *Hadeeths* using different chains of narrators so as to strengthen the various texts, if applicable. They also include the *Fatawa*, or religious opinions, of the Prophet's companions (﷠) and the two successive generations, as well as, weak *Hadeeths*.

There are more than three-hundred major *Hadeeth* Collections. As stated before, *Hadeeth* Collections contain repetitions of various Prophetic Statements and actions contained in the other books of *Hadeeth*, by using various independent or repetitive chains of narrators. They also contain statements from the Prophet's companions and the successive generations of scholars with regards to various aspects of Islam. They also include weak and unsubstantiated narrations. However, while *Hadeeth* narrations found in various *Hadeeth* Collections are repetitious, the entire *Sunnah* is found in them collectively and answers any question regarding the Islamic religion that any person may have.

Forty-Ninth: *Sahih al-Bukhari;* Example of *Sunnah* Collections.

One month before he died, Imam al-Bukhari said, "I collected Hadeeth from one thousand and eighty men (teachers); every one of them is a narrator of Hadeeth."[72]

---

[72] [Asqalani, Ibn `Hajar. *Fat`h-ul Bari bi Shar`h-i Sahih-i-l-Bukhari* (Vol., 1, Pg., 44) & Dhahabi, Shams ad-Deen. *Siyar-u A`lami an-Nubalaa* (Vol. 12, Pg., 395).

Continue on next page...

Imam al-Bukhari was born in Bukhara, in today's Uzbekistan, 194 years after the Prophet's *Hijrah*, which occurred in 623 CE. Bukhara was conquered by the great Muslim leader, Qutaibah Ibn Muslim (48-96AH/668-714), in the 90th year of *Hijrah*[73] which coincided with the year 708CE. Thus, when Imam al-Bukhari was born, Bukhara had already been an Islamic city for more than a hundred years. It was also a center for Islamic Knowledge, such as Knowledge of *Hadeeth*. Numerous companions and *Tabi'un* scholars had migrated to and resided in the new Islamic areas, thus, transferring knowledge of the *Quran* and *Sunnah* to the farthest parts of the Islamic World. Travel between Islamic areas was safe, affordable, exciting, beneficial and quite widespread. At the early age of sixteen, Imam al-Bukhari had traveled to major cities of the Muslim World.

Bukhari's Biography

His name was: Muhammad, Ibn (son of) Isma`eel, Ibn Ibrahim, Ibn al-Mughirah, Ibn Bardizbah, which means, 'the farmer'. Al-Mughirah, who used to be a *Majusi*, Fire-Worshipper, became Muslim during the reign of al-Yaman al-Ju`fi, Governor of Bukhara. Al-Bukhari's *Kunyah*, or title, is Abu Abdillah.

As al-Bukhari himself reported, his father, Isma`eel Ibn Ibrahim, sought knowledge of *Hadeeth*. Imam Adh-Dhahabi, a major Muslim Scholar and Historian, said that al-Bukhari said, "My father heard [*Hadeeth* narrations] from Malik Ibn Anas, saw Hammad Ibn Zaid (98-179AH/716-795), and shook both hands of [Abdullah] Ibn al-Mubarak (118-181AH/736-797)." *The three*

Continued from previous page...
Bukhari's biography reported in this book was mainly taken from adh-Dhahabi's, *Siyar-u A`lami an-Nubalaa* (Vol. 12, Pg., 391-471); Asqalani's, *Fat`h-ul Bari*, was also used.]

[73] [Dhahabi, Shams ad-Deen. *Siyar-u A`lami an-Nubalaa* [4:410-411].]

scholars mentioned here are some of the most respected scholars of Islam, especially in the knowledge of Hadeeth.

Imam Muhammad Ibn Abi Hatim reported that he asked al-Bukhari about how he started learning knowledge and Bukhari replied, by saying, "I was made [by Allah] to like memorizing *Hadeeth* when I was in *Kuttab*." When asked how old he was then, he said, "Ten years old, or younger." The *Kuttab* is a simple school where young Muslim children attend classes to learn basic Arabic, math, the proper method of reciting *Quran* and learn to memorize *Quran*. Often, young children would memorize the entire *Quran* at an early age, even before they reach the age of ten. This method of teaching *Quran* still thrives today in various parts of the Islamic World.

Al-Bukhari said, "When I was sixteen years of age, I had already memorized the books of [Abdullah] Ibn al-Mubarak and Waki` [Ibn al-Jarra`h] ... then traveled to Makkah with my mother and Ahmad, my brother. After I made *Hajj*, my brother traveled back with my mother and I remained behind seeking [Knowledge of *Hadeeth*]." Al-Bukhari had already heard *Hadeeth* narrations in Bukhara before he traveled to Makkah.

As stated, al-Bukhari had numerous teachers with whom he learned all aspects of Islamic Knowledge and from whom he heard *Hadeeth* narrations. It is not possible to list all of Bukhari's *Shuyukh* (teachers) here. A partial list will be sufficient. Only one teacher will be mentioned from some of the areas where Bukhari sought knowledge of `Hadeeth.

In Balkh, today's Afghanistan, al-Bukhari heard *Hadeeth* narrations from Makki Ibn Ibrahim (126-214AH/743-829); in Marw, today's Turkmenistan, he heard *Hadeeth* from Ali Ibn al-Hasan Ibn Shaqiq (137-215AH/754-830); in Naisabur, Persia, from Ya`hya Ibn Ya`hya (142-226AH/759-840); in ar-Rai, today's Persia, from Ibrahim Ibn Musa (d. 230AH/844); in Baghdad, Iraq, from Suraij Ibn an-Nu`man (d. 227AH/841); in al-Basra, Iraq, from adh-Dha`hhak Ibn Makhlad, also known as Abu Asim an-Nabeel (122-212AH/739-827); in al-Kufah, Iraq, from Talq Ibn Ghannam (d.

211AH/826); in Makkah, Hijaz, from Abdullah Ibn az-Zubair Al-`Humaidi (d. 219AH/834); in Madinah, Hijaz, from Abdul Aziz al-Uwaisi (d. 220AH/835); in Egypt from Sa`eed Ibn Abi Maryam (144-224AH/761-838); in ash-Sham (Syria) from Ali Ibn Ayyash (143-219AH/760-834), and so forth. *Al-Bukhari learned with more than a thousand teachers; this list is very brief compared to the entire list of teachers with whom al-Bukhari learned Hadeeth and other aspects of Islamic knowledge.*

Every one of al-Bukhari's teachers had a verifiable biography collected in books of *Rijal* (men), which focus on male and female narrators of *Hadeeth*. All of Bukhari's listed teachers, and as stated, only a very small number of Bukhari's teachers is mentioned here, are well-known narrators whose trustworthiness, state of mind, character and power of memory can be verified relying on what their contemporary scholars and students said about them, in addition to the books they wrote and the legacy they left behind.

The biography of every one of these teachers also includes mention of their teachers and students, and their teachers and students, and so forth. The chain continues expanding in this manner the closer or farther Muslims get to the time of the Prophet (ﷺ) and his companions (رضي الله عنهم). A unique, distinct Islamic knowledge called, '*Ilm ar-Rijal* (Knowledge of men)', was developed for the purpose of studying the trustworthiness of narrators of *Hadeeth*, male and female.

Imam Shams ad-Din adh-Dhahabi (673-748AH/1274-1347), one of the major Muslim Scholars of *Hadeeth* and Islamic History, continued his biography on al-Bukhari, by saying that among al-Bukhari's teachers who reported *Hadeeth* from the *Tabi`in* [the second generation of Islam] were Abu Asim an-Nabeel (122-212AH/739-827), Makki Ibn Ibrahim (126-214AH/743-829), Abu al-Mughirah Abdul Quddus Ibn al-Hajjaj (130-212AH/747-827), among others. *Consequently, in some of the Hadeeth narrations al-Bukhari collected, there were only three people between him and the*

Prophet of Allah (ﷺ); *this type of chain of narrators is called, Thulathiyyat* (literally means, 'threes').

Numerous scholars collected *Hadeeth* from al-Bukhari, such as these famous Collectors of *Hadeeth*: Muslim Ibn al-`Hajjaj al-Qushairi[74] (204-261AH/819-874); Muhammad Ibn `Esa at-Tirmidhi (210-279AH/825-892); Abu Hatim ar-Razi (195-277AH/810-890); Abu Bakr Ibn Abi ad-Dunya (b. 208AH/823); Abu Bakr Ibn Abi Asim (206-278AH/821-891); Abu Bakr Ibn Khuzaimah (223-311AH/837-923), among others. *The scholars mentioned here are also major Hadeeth Collectors in their own right.* Imam adh-Dhahabi said that his teacher, Imam Abu al-`Hajjaj al-Mizzi (654-742AH/1256-1341), collected the names of al-Bukhari's teachers and students in a volume by itself.

Imam adh-Dhahabi reported that ninety thousand (**90,000**) students heard *Sahih al-Bukhari* being recited to them. Many of these students transmitted al-Bukhari's entire *Sahih*. Al-Bukhari said that it took him sixteen years to finish collecting his *Sahih*; he did not add a *Hadeeth* to the *Sahih* until after washing by making *Ghusl* then performing a two *Rak'ah* prayer.[75] Bukhari said that he only included authentic *Hadeeths* in his *Sahih*. He also said that he left out other authentic *Hadeeths* so the book would not become larger in size.

Al-Bukhari memorized more than six hundred thousand narrations (**600,000**).[76] Imam Adh-Dhahabi added that among the narrations al-Bukhari memorized were two hundred thousand unauthentic narrations (**200,000**).

Imam Ibn Hajar al-Asqalani said that scholars of *Hadeeth* in Baghdad tested al-Bukhari's memory by asking ten men to each recite ten *Hadeeth* narrations to al-Bukhari. However, the chains of narrators and texts for all one hundred *Hadeeths* were intentionally

---

[74] [Muslim collected his own *Sahih* Collection, popularly known as, *Sahih Muslim*, which, along with, *Sahih al-Bukhari*, are called 'The Two Sahihs']

[75] [Dhahabi, Shams ad-Deen. *Siyar-u A`lami an-Nubalaa* (Vol. 12, Pg., 404-405).]

[76] [Asqalani, Ibn `Hajar. *Fat`h-ul-Bari: The Introduction* (Pg., 683).]

switched. After the ten men finished reciting all of the hundred *Hadeeths* assigned to them, al-Bukhari repeated every *Hadeeth* they recited in the order it was recited to the man who recited it. He then recited to each of the ten men the correct text and chain of narrators for the *Hadeeths* they recited, one *Hadeeth* at a time. The audience was astonished and attested and admitted to al-Bukhari's immense memorizing ability.

Al-Jami` as-Sahih (Sahih al-Bukhari)

Al-Jami` as-Sahih, also known as, **Sahih al-Bukhari**, is al-Bukhari's famous collection of authentic *Hadeeths*. It comprises more than four thousand different *Hadeeths*, close to seven thousand and six hundred *Hadeeths* when repeated *Hadeeths* are counted.[77]

As stated, *al-Jami` as-Sahih* was taught to more than ninety thousand pupils who heard the collection, *Hadeeth* by *Hadeeth*, narrated to them by al-Bukhari himself.[78] During that era, *Hadeeth* Scholars used to teach *Hadeeth* narrations in designated, open areas to students, who would gather by the thousands to hear *Hadeeth* narrations. Men were assigned to loudly repeat the statements they heard from the teacher, for pupils sitting in back rows, so they could hear clearly.

An Example of Bukhari's *Hadeeth* Narrations

This is an example of Bukhari's *Hadeeth* narrations. The entire chain of narration for this *Hadeeth* is mentioned in Arabic and English, followed by a brief comment on the narrators of the *Hadeeth*. In this *Hadeeth*, which is *Hadeeth* number 106, there are only three narrators between Bukhari and the Prophet of Allah (ﷺ).

---

[77] [Nawawi, Ya`hya Ibn Sharaf. *Tah-dheebu-l-Asmaa-i wal-Lughat* [1/75/1].]
[78] [Asqalani, Ibn `Hajar. *Fat`h-ul-Bari: The Introduction* (Pg., 686).]

Al-Bukhari said,

حَدَّثَنَا مَكِّيُّ بْنُ إِبْرَاهِيمَ قَالَ حَدَّثَنَا يَزِيدُ بْنُ أَبِي عُبَيْدٍ عَنْ سَلَمَةَ قَالَ سَمِعْتُ النَّبِيَّ ﷺ يَقُولُ: " مَنْ يَقُلْ عَلَيَّ مَا لَمْ أَقُلْ فَلْيَتَبَوَّأْ مَقْعَدَهُ مِنَ النَّارِ "

"Makki Ibn Ibrahim narrated to us, by saying, 'Yazid Ibn Abi Ubaid narrated to us that, Salamah said, 'I heard the Prophet (ﷺ) say, *'He who ascribes to me a statement that I did not say, let him assume his* [assured] *seat in the Hellfire.'*"

The four narrators of this *Hadeeth* are:
1. **Muhammad Ibn Isma`eel al-Bukhari** (194-256AH/817-879);
2. **Makki Ibn Ibrahim** (126-214AH/743-829), Bukhari's teacher;
3. **Yazid Ibn Abi Ubaid** (d. 147AH/764), Makki's teacher;
4. **Salamah Ibn al-Akwa'** (d. 74AH/693), Yazid's teacher, and the Prophet's close companion.
    a. According to Imam adh-Dhahabi, Salamah (﷜) was in his nineties when he died.
    b. Yazid Ibn Abi `Ubaid, a trustworthy narrator of *Hadeeth*, was one of Salamah's close associates and young pupils. Yazid lived long after Salamah and benefited Muslims from his narrations from Salamah.
    c. Makki Ibn Ibrahim, a trustworthy scholar of *Hadeeth*, is Yazid Ibn Abi Uybaid's student and al-Bukhari's teacher in this *Hadeeth*.

Knowledge of *Hadeeth* survived and still exists in the present time through the ongoing scientific movement to study texts of *Hadeeths* and their chains of narrators to determine authentic *Hadeeths* and to expose weak and fabricated ones. Since all of the texts and chains of narrators necessary to transmit the Prophet's *Hadeeth* Statements were recorded in writing in the early Islamic Era, scholars of later generations concentrated on studying and analyzing the texts and the chains of narrators that were already recorded in earlier books.

Consequently, even in the present time, this knowledge is available to scholars and students of knowledge, who can still study *Hadeeth* narrations and conduct scientific analysis of their texts and chains of narrators to determine authenticity or lack of it. This scientific effort relies heavily on the beneficial work of early Muslim Scholars who recorded their findings in books and manuscripts.

This is how the Prophet's Sunnah was protected, its knowledge accurately inherited from one generation to the next generation, until it reached us as fresh and viable as the day Allah's Prophet (ﷺ) spoke it, practiced it and explained it.

Fiftieth: This is the legacy of Muhammad (ﷺ), the Prophet of Mercy; what this book contains is only part of why Muslims love and respect Muhammad (ﷺ) more than they love and respect any other human being.

When Allah (ﷻ) sent Muhammad (ﷺ) as His Final and Last Prophet and Messenger, the Arab Nation was weak, poor and divided into hundreds of tribes, each fiercely independent and largely nomadic, living in one of the harshest environments on earth. There were few large villages in Arabia, while the Arabs who lived in Iraq, Syria, Yemen and Egypt were under the governance of either the Roman or Persian Empires.

After Allah (ﷻ) sent Muhammad (ﷺ), the Prophet of Mercy, and for the first time in their long history, Arabs became united and had a sense of purpose and belonging to one Nation, the Islamic Nation. The Islamic Nation established a unique civilization that was built around the Arabic *Quran* and *Sunnah*, but included in it mighty nations that accepted Islam freely and willingly, from North Africa to India and from Turkey to Yemen, including the African Horn.

In these times, Islam exists in every populated continent on earth. More than 49 countries have either a majority or a near

Muhammad's Role in Islam

majority population of Muslims. More than one-fifth of humanity now attests to Islam, which continues to grow faster than any other religion on earth. The *Quran* and *Sunnah* are the foundation of this great *Ummah* (Nation); these two resources fueled one of the greatest civilizations to have ever flourished in the history of mankind. The Arabic language was no longer the property of Arabs alone. Arabic became the language of Islam, especially since all the original resources of Islam are written, and still found, in Arabic. Also, almost the entire generation that learned Islam from its Prophet (ﷺ) and transmitted it to the next generation was Arab.

Only a few companions were non-Arab, yet, they spoke Arabic as fluently as any Arab and were righteous Muslims. Great nations joined the *Ummah* of Muhammad (ﷺ), and by freely joining the Islamic Nation, they immediately became brothers and sisters to every other Muslim and equal to them before Allah (ﷻ) and then before man. The scale with which to weigh men and women no longer was tied to their origin or race, but to their piety and righteousness. Arabs had no virtue above non-Arabs; righteous Muslims, whether Arab or non-Arab, always had a virtue above the non-righteous who included the Prophet's own uncle, Abu Lahab, who opposed Muhammad (ﷺ), until death.

By visiting a Masjid, any Masjid, one will notice that those who attend the congregational prayer come from every race and every cultural background, standing in line next to each other, praying behind one Imam, who is the leader of the prayer, praying to the One and Only Lord and Creator of all that exists and striving to follow the *Sunnah* of Islam's Prophet, Muhammad (ﷺ). All this was possible by the sending of Muhammad (ﷺ),

﴿ وَمَآ أَرْسَلْنَٰكَ إِلَّا رَحْمَةً لِّلْعَٰلَمِينَ ﴾

{*And We have sent you* (O, Muhammad ﷺ) *not but as a mercy for the 'Âlamîn* (all that exists)} (21:107).

Introduction to: Muhammad (ﷺ), The Prophet of Mercy

The transformation that occurred in the lives of the Arabs and other Muslims through Muhammad (ﷺ), Allah's Final and Last Prophet and Messenger, is best described by a short statement reported from Umar Ibn al-Khattab. But first, here are some brief words that describe the three persons involved in the narration to be mentioned.

1. **Abu Bakr** (ؓ): The Prophet's closest friend and disciple, father-in-law, minister, confidant, associate and immediate successor.
2. **Umar Ibn al-Khattab** (ؓ): The Prophet's second closest friend, father-in-law, minister, confidant and close associate; he succeeded Abu Bakr as the *Khaleefah*, Leader of the Islamic State.
3. **Bilal Ibn Raba`h** (ؓ): One of the Prophet's major companions, close friends, and one of the earliest Muslims.

Imam Ibn Qayyim al-Jauziyyah said, "Bilal Ibn Raba`h (ؓ) was also tortured severely [by the pagans of Makkah], because he believed in Allah (ﷻ). While Bilal's life became insignificant to his people, Bilal himself felt that his life became insignificant to him in Allah's Sake[79]. The more the pagans tortured him, the more Bilal repeated this statement, '`A`hadun, A`had (Allah is One, Allah is One)'" (A *Sahih Hadeeth*; *Sahih Ibn Majah* [122]).

Bilal (ؓ) had several major deficiencies in the eyes of Arab pagans, he was a black, non-Arab, Ethiopian slave. Bilal (ؓ) found in Islam the ultimate freedom from the chains of the pagan system of oppression, idol-worshipping and racism. He embraced a religion whose Prophet, peace be upon him, declared,

" وَالنَّاسُ بَنُو آدَمَ وَخَلَقَ اللهُ آدَمَ مِنْ تُرَابٍ "

---

[79] [i.e., Bilal decided to remain Muslim whether he was tortured or killed in Allah's Sake]

"All of mankind is the children of Adam, and Allah created Adam from dust" (A Hasan Hadeeth; Sahih al-Jami`⁸⁰ [7867]).

The Prophet, peace be upon him, also said,

" يَا أَيُّهَا النَّاسُ أَلاَ إِنَّ رَبَّكُمْ وَاحِدٌ وَإِنَّ أَبَاكُمْ وَاحِدٌ أَلاَ لاَ فَضْلَ لِعَرَبِيٍّ عَلَى أَعْجَمِيٍّ وَلاَ لِعَجَمِيٍّ عَلَى عَرَبِيٍّ وَلاَ لأَحْمَرَ عَلَى أَسْوَدَ وَلاَ أَسْوَدَ عَلَى أَحْمَرَ إِلاَّ بِالتَّقْوَى "

"O, People! Verily, your Lord is One (Allah), *and your father is one* (Adam). *Verily, an Arab has no virtue above a non-Arab, nor a non-Arab has a virtue above an Arab, nor does a red person have a virtue above a black person, nor a black person above a red person, except by fear and obedience to Allah."* (A Sahih Hadeeth; as-Sahih al-Musnad⁸¹ [1536]]

Bilal (ﷺ) won his ultimate freedom by embracing Islam, and won his physical freedom by the hand of the Prophet's trusted and closest friend and disciple, Abu Bakr (ﷺ), the father of `Aishah (ﷺ), the Prophet's beloved wife. As he did for the benefit of many other weak Muslims, Abu Bakr bought Bilal's freedom with his own money and set him free. Bilal had suffered severe torture by the disbelievers of Makkah.

After the death of the Prophet (ﷺ) and Abu Bakr (ﷺ), `Umar Ibn al-Khattab (ﷺ), the Prophet's second closest friend, who belonged to an honorable sub-tribe of Quraish, became the Caliph of the Islamic State, then the most prosperous and the strongest

---

⁸⁰ [*Al-Jami` as-Sagheer*: Imam Jalal ad-Deen as-Suyuti (849-911AH/1445-1505) collected this vast collection of Prophetic *Hadeeths*.
Imam Nasir ad-Deen al-Albani separated the *Sahih* (authentic) *Hadeeths* found in, *al-Jami` as-Sagheer*, from the *Dha`eef* (weak) *Hadeeths* found therein; al-Albani titled the first book, *Sahih al-Jami` as-Sagheer*, and titled the second book, *Dha`eef al-Jami` as-Sagheer*.]

⁸¹ [Wadi`i, Muqbil Ibn Hadi. *As-Sahih al-Musnad*.
Shaikh Muqbil Ibn Hadi al-Wadi`i (1352-1422AH/1933-2001) was one of the Imams of *Sunnah* in our time.]

nation in the world. `Umar was sitting with a group of the Prophet's companions (ﷺ) when Bilal passed by them, greeted them and went his way. With all the love and respect `Umar (ﷺ) and the rest of Muslims had for Bilal (ﷺ), `Umar issued this outstanding statement:

"Abu Bakr was our *Sayyid* (chief; leader; master) and he freed our *Sayyid* (meaning Bilal)" (*Bukhari* [3471]).

Let this be a gift to those who still do not understand the power of Islam and the profound effect it has on the hearts of those who believe in it. Let this be a gift to those who, in this twenty-first century, still think of other people in terms of color and racial background,

﴿ يَٰٓأَيُّهَا ٱلنَّاسُ إِنَّا خَلَقْنَٰكُم مِّن ذَكَرٍ وَأُنثَىٰ وَجَعَلْنَٰكُمْ شُعُوبًا وَقَبَآئِلَ لِتَعَارَفُوٓا۟ إِنَّ أَكْرَمَكُمْ عِندَ ٱللَّهِ أَتْقَىٰكُمْ ۚ إِنَّ ٱللَّهَ عَلِيمٌ خَبِيرٌ ﴾

{*O, Mankind! We have created you from a male* (Adam) *and a female* (`Hawwa [Eve]), *and made you into nations and tribes, that you may know one another. Verily, the most honorable of you with Allâh is that* (believer) *who has at-Taqwâ* (piety)].} (49:13)

List of References

1. Albani, Nasir ad-Deen (1988). *Sahih Sunan Abi Dawud*. Maktab at-Tarbiyah al-Arabi.
2. ---. *Sahih Sunan an-Nasaii*. ---.
3. ---. *Sahih Sunan Ibn Majah*. ---.
4. ---. *Sahih Sunan at-Tirmidhi*. ---.
5. ---. *Dhilal al-Jannah fi Takhreej as-Sunnah*. Beirut, Lebanon: Al-Maktab al-Islami.
6. ---. *Sahih al-Jami` as-Sagheer*. Beirut, Lebanon: Al-Maktab Al-Islami.
7. ---. *Manzilat as-Sunnah fi-l-Islam wa-Bayan Annahu la-Yustaghna `Anha bi-l-Quran* (Status of the *Sunnah* in Islam and Proving that the *Quran* Alone Does not Suffice [for Muslims]). Kuwait: Ad-Dar as-Salafiyyah.
8. --- (1995). *Al-Hadithu `Hujjatun bi-Nafsihi fi al-A`hkami wa-l-`Aqa-id* (The `Hadith is Proof Itself in Matters of Law and Creed) (Jalal Abualrub, Tarns.). Miami, FL: The Dar for Islamic Heritage).
9. ---. *Sahih at-Targheeb wa-t-Tarheeb*. Riyadh, KSA: Maktabat al-Ma`arif.
10. ---. *Silsilat al-A`hadeeth as-Sahihah*. Riyadh, KSA: Maktabat al-Ma`arif.
11. Asqalani, Ahmad Ibn Ali Ibn Hajar. *Fat`h al-Bari Shar`h Sahih al-Bukhari*.
12. Bukhari, Muhammad Ibn Isma`eel (1987). *Al-Jamiu` as-Sahih (Sahih al-Bukhari)*. Beirut, Lebanon: Dar al-Qalam.
13. ---. *Tarikh al-Bukhari*.
14. Dhahabi, Shams ad-Deen (1990). *Siyar-u A`lami an-Nubalaa*. Beirut, Lebanon: Muassasat ar-Risalah.
15. Hilali, Muhammad Taqi-ud-Din & Khan, Muhammad Mu`hsin (1996). *Interpretation of the Meanings of the Noble Quran*. Riyadh, KSA: Darussalam Publishers and Distributors.
16. ---. *Interpretation of the Meanings of Sahih al-Bukhari*. Riyadh, KSA: Darussalam Publishers and Distributors.
17. Ibn Abdul Barr, Abu Umar. *At-Tamheed lima fi-l-Muwattaa mina-l-Ma`ani wal-Asaneed*.

18. Ibn Anas, Malik. *Al-Muwatta*.
19. Ibn al-`Arabi, Abu Bakr. *A`hkamu al-Quran*.
20. Ibn Hanbal, Ahmad. *Al-Musnad*
21. Ibn Kathir, Isam`eel Ibn `Amr. *Tafsir Ibn Kathir*.
22. Ibn Taimiyyah, Ahmad Ibn Abdul `Haleem. *Majmu` al-Fatawa*.
23. Nawawi, Ya`hya Ibn Sharaf. *Shar`h Sahih Muslim*. Beirut, Lebanon: Dar al-Qalam.
24. ---. *Tah-dheebu-l-Asmaa-i wal-Lughat*.
25. Qushairi, Muslim Ibn al-`Hajjaj (1972). *Sahih Muslim*. Dar I`hyaa at-Turath al-`Arabi.
26. Saqr, Abdul Badee` (1992). *At-Tajweedu wa-`Ulumu al-Quran*. Beirut, Lebanon: Al-Maktab al-Islami.
27. Shakir, Ahmad. *Umdatu at-Tafsir*.
28. Wadi`i, Muqbil Ibn Hadi. *As-Sahih al-Musnad mimma laisa fi as-Sahihain*. Maktabat Dar-al-Quds.

Selected Books Translated by Jalal Abualrub

Madinah Publishers and Distributors:
- Volumes: One, Two, Three and Four of the English Translation of the Encyclopedia of Prophetic Tradition, *Zad-ul Ma`ad fi Hadyi Khairi al-`Ibad*, by Imam in Qayyim al-Jauziyyah;
- *Holy Wars, Crusades, Jihad*; authored by Jalal Abualrub.
- *Biography of Muhammad Ibn Abdul Wahhab*; authored by Jalal Abualrub; A 700-page historical study taken from more than 300 different western and Islamic resources on an important part of the history of Arabs in the eighteenth century.

Books Jalal Abualrub translated for Darussalam Publishers and Distributors (www.dar-us-salam.com)
- Chapters (*Juzu*) 1-10, 12, 13, 25- 27 of, *Tafsir Ibn Kathir*;
- Chapters 1 & 2 of, *Selected Friday Sermons*, (chapters 3 & 4 were translated by Ibrahim Ezghair);
- *Pillars of Islam*, by Abdullah Ibn Jabrin;
- *Silent Moments*, by Abdul-Malik Al-Qasim;
- *How to Achieve Happiness*, by Abdur-Rahman As-Sa`di;
- *Healing With The Medicine of the Prophet*, by Imam Ibn Qayyim Al-Jauziyyah;
- *The Seerah (Biography) of the Prophet*, by al-Mubarakpuri (Not Published Yet)
- *Establish the Prayers & the Prize is Paradise*, by Abdul-Malik Al-Qasim.

Books Jalal Abualrub translated for Dar at-Turath al-Islami
(The Dar for Islamic Heritage; Orlando, Florida, USA)
- *Innovation, and its Evil Effects*, by Sali'h al Fozan;
- *Rights Basic to the Natural Human Constitution*, by Muhammad al Uthaymeen;
- *The Hadith is Proof Itself in Belief and Laws*, by Nasirudden al Albani;
- *Explaining the Pillars of Iman*, by Mohammad al Uthaymeen;
- *Marriage in Islam*, by Abdurrahman Abdul-Khaliq;
- *Kitab Al Ikhlas (Book of Sincerity)*, by Husain al Awaysha;
- *Basics & Benefits from the Forty Hadith Nawawi*, by Nathim Sultan.